# Time Management

*Creative Leadership Series*

*Assimilating New Members,* Lyle E. Schaller
*Beginning a New Pastorate,* Robert G. Kemper
*The Care and Feeding of Volunteers,* Douglas W. Johnson
*Creative Stewardship,* Richard B. Cunningham
*Time Management,* Speed B. Leas
*Your Church Can Be Healthy,* C. Peter Wagner
*Leading Churches Through Change,* Douglas Alan Walrath
*Building an Effective Youth Ministry,* Glenn E. Ludwig
*Preaching and Worship in the Small Church,*
William Willimon and Robert L. Wilson
*Church Growth,*
Donald McGavran and George G. Hunter, III
*The Pastor's Wife Today,* Donna Sinclair
*The Small Town Church,* Peter J. Surrey
*Strengthening the Adult Sunday School Class,* Dick Murray
*Church Advertising,* Steve Dunkin

# Time Management

Speed B. Leas

*Creative Leadership Series*
*Lyle E. Schaller, Editor*

Abingdon
Nashville

TIME MANAGEMENT



Sixth Printing 1981



**Library of Congress Cataloging in Publication Data**

LEAS, SPEED, 1937–
Time management.
(Creative leadership series)
1. Church management. 2. Time allocation. I. Title. II. Series.
BV652.9.L42 254 78-8628

**ISBN 0-687-42120-9**



MANUFACTURED BY THE PARTHENON PRESS AT NASHVILLE, TENNESSEE, UNITED STATES OF AMERICA

This book is dedicated to my father,
Nathaniel Newcomer Leas, and my mother,
Ernestine Burum Leas, who believed that
"you always have enough time for what
you really want to do."

And which of you by being anxious
can add a cubit to his span of life?

**Luke 12:25**

There is no living when you're nagging time
and stunting every second with your will.

**Marya Mannes,**
"Time, Gentlemen, Please"

# Foreword

Various surveys of pastors have emphasized repeatedly two points. First, a large proportion of ministers indicate their seminary training did not provide adequate preparation for the administrative and leadership responsibilities that occupy so much of their day. Second, many express a high level of frustration over their inability to use their time more productively.

The Creative Leadership Series is directed toward the first of these concerns. This series of paperback books has been designed to strengthen, reinforce, and expand the competence of congregational leaders, both lay and clergy, in several areas of administration and leadership. A widely used and simple phrase describing the role of a leader is *leaders initiate.* This is a central thrust in each of the books in this series. Bob Kemper's volume is filled with insights and ideas for the minister moving to a new pastorate and for the lay leaders in the congregation about to receive a new pastor. My contribution to this series is based on the assumption that the key issue in the assimilation of new members into the fellowship of the congregation is the willingness of the pastor and the lay leadership to take the initiative in causing that to happen. That responsibility rests with the members and the pastor, not with the new member!

Doug Johnson has opened up a whole series of approaches by which the network of volunteers in the church, or in any other voluntary organization, can be strengthened and expanded. In his book he details very carefully the importance of leaders taking the initiative in the care and feeding of the volunteer lay workers in the church.

In his volume on stewardship, Dick Cunningham provides theological, biblical, and practical insights for congregational leaders who seek to strengthen the concept of the stewardship of all of life.

This volume by Speed Leas speaks to both of the points mentioned earlier. In this book the author explains how each of us must take the initiative if we are to be good stewards of the hours God has given each of us. Taking the initiative requires an active rather than a passive stance by the individual. A passive posture means that other people will define our role, set our priorities, and allocate our time for us. Leaders initiate! That means that a leader takes the initiative in the allocation of his or her time. It does not mean a person cannot be sensitive and responsive to the needs of others. It does mean, however, that we have to take the initiative in setting our own priorities.

This book is filled with creative suggestions on how to do it. It is not simply a book that depresses the reader by a long list of "oughts." It is a book filled with creative "hows." These range from the identification of the compulsive-worker syndrome and how to deal creatively with that compulsion, to the procrastinator who has a high level of competence in postponing time-consuming obligations.

In one of the pioneering contributions in this volume the author identifies the conflicting demands of a variety of roles as a basic cause of the frustration over time management by church leaders. He suggests several ways by which each person can turn this frustrating conflict into a creative means of identifying strengths and building on these strengths.

Perhaps the most seriously neglected dimension on the studies of the work load of ministers is the underemployed pastor. This is not a rare phenomenon. The fourth chapter in this volume identifies and describes this situation. More significantly, Mr. Leas describes how the underemployed pastor can turn this chapter in a ministerial career into a highly creative and very productive period.

This volume should be of help to all creative leaders in the churches.

Lyle E. Schaller
Yokefellow Institute

# Contents

# Introduction

The title of this book implies that it is possible to manage time. That is not true. Time is not manageable. However, it is possible to manage *oneself* in time and to be responsive to circumstances as they arise. It is these two themes to which this book is addressed: how to choose to live in the time that you have and how to be responsive to the fact that "this is the day which the Lord has made" (Ps. 118:24).

Time is a totally inelastic quantity. It cannot be added to; it cannot be changed; it cannot be subtracted from; it cannot be stretched or shrunk; and *it cannot be saved!* The time you have to live is one of the things in your life over which you have no control. Your time is a pure gift. You didn't earn it; you don't deserve it; you didn't choose it; and you can't give it up. Even if you did choose to leave this life (give up your time), that too would be futile, for you have been given the gift of everlasting life. In a roundabout way Dorothy Parker makes this point in her poem *The Flaw in Paganism:*

> Drink, and dance and laugh and lie,
> Love, the reeling midnight through,
> For tomorrow we shall die!
> (But alas, we never do.)

Time is the gift that has been given to you and me and has a very special holiness from our Hebrew tradition. Abraham Heschel suggests that time rather than space is seen as holy. This is what is unique about our religious roots:

> "And God blessed the seventh *day* and made it *holy.*" There is no reference in the record of creation to any object in space that would be endowed with the quality of holiness.
>
> This is a radical departure from accustomed religious thinking. The mythical mind would expect that, after heaven and earth have been established, God would create a holy place—a holy mountain or a holy spring—whereupon a sanctuary is to be established. Yet it seems as if to the Bible it is *holiness in time,* the Sabbath, which comes first.[1]

## Is This Book for You?

While I do not claim to be able to write about how to manage time, the title of the book is accurate to the extent that the book is in the genre now commonly called "time-management literature." It is a book that deals with those common time-management problems of church, government, business, and educational executives (and a pastor, by the way, is an executive by the common definition of that term: "a person or body charged with or skilled in administrative work.") The book will discuss four time-management problems found in the professional ministry: compulsiveness, procrastination, role conflict, and lack of enough to do. In addition, I have included a list of labor-saving devices (a term I much prefer to "ways to save time") that I have found useful in my professional ministry.

In order to help you determine whether you may be among those to whom this book is addressed, here are vignettes of the four time-management problems:

## Compulsiveness

Ira Jones works, works, works. Ever since he was in seminary, where he almost never left the books, he has become a "Johnnie one note" of the ministry. His one note is work. He goes to a different church meeting every night. When there is no meeting at his own church, he is at an ecumenical meeting or at one with his denomination. Saturdays are taken up with weddings and last-minute preparations of the sermon for Sunday. On one of those rare occasions when his family is able to talk him into going to a movie, they know that it will have to be relevant and have many possibilities for sermon illustrations. No James Bond flicks for Ira.

Ira's problems not only relate to himself. They also affect his family. He gets little rest and feels driven and exhausted most of the time. His family rarely sees him, and when they do, it is usually in the pulpit or at a time when he needs one of them to serve as a substitute Sunday school teacher. Further, he has problems in relating to other people. They see him as consumed with his own work and his own importance, and they feel reluctant to interrupt him or bring their little problems to him. He protests that he has an open-door policy and that anyone who wants to see him knows exactly where he can be found at every minute. This may be true, but when you want a minute to talk, he looks at his watch. When one of the kids in the choir went into the hospital for a tonsilectomy, nobody told Ira because they didn't want to bother him with such a little thing. When you ride with him in the car to go to the next town for a conference on Christian education, he brings a book to read.

If some of this sounds familiar, you may want to read chapter 1.

**Procrastination**

9:00 to 9:15 A.M.

I've dusted my desk and I've wound up my watch,
I've tightened (then loosened) my belt by a notch.
I've polished my glasses, removed a small speck.
I've looked at my check stubs to check on a check,
I've searched for my tweezers and pulled out a hair,
I've opened a window to let in some air,
I've straightened a picture, I've swatted a fly,
I've shifted the tie clip that clips down my tie,
I've sharpened each pencil till sharp as a dirk . . .
I've run out of reasons for not starting to work.

Richard Armour

If this poem sounds like the way you get down to preparing a sermon, you may want to read chapter 2. Other examples of procrastination include putting off unpleasant or large projects until the last minute, not doing some important things at all (like calling on members, for instance), making mental excuses for not doing something until later, and forgetting other things until it's almost or is too late to do anything about it. (Remember that elderly couple you were going to have over for dinner before they went to the rest home?)

## Role Conflict

Kathy Buckminster is a Presbyterian minister who has just read the *Pastoral Activities Index,* published jointly by The United Presbyterian Church in the U.S.A. and the Presbyterian Church in the U.S., which lists 8 roles for the clergy (director of worship, facilitator of pastoral care, leader and interpreter of mission, coordinator of church education, facilitator of parish/community relationships, administrator, member of presbytery, and member of the profession). Under each of the 8 roles listed there is an average of 5 tasks per role, and these tasks are broken down into 1 and 7 subtasks each. There were 192 roles, tasks, and subtasks listed in all!

But that is just half of it. Not only has her denomination defined an impossible task for her, the congregation of which she is the pastor has done so as well. They drew up a job description for her that included a number of specific pastoral activities that they expect her to perform in the normal routine of her ministry. But many members of the parish seem to lay on more than the job description calls for in the first place. They keep getting sick, going to the hospital, wanting to have weddings, demanding her presence at women's circle meetings, and expecting her to be at community events. Not only that, her husband and three-year-old son ask for her attention and presence in their lives. When does she find time for her own private and devotional life? She feels overwhelmed by it all.

If Kathy's problems sound familiar to you, read chapter 3.

### Not Enough to Do

This book has been cleverly written so that those of you who do not have enough to do in the professional ministry can buy it but pretend that your real interest is in the first three chapters. No one has to know that you have read chapter 4 if you don't underline any of the sentences or write notes in the margin.

Richard Beeker is a pastor without enough to do. He graduated from Yale Divinity School last year, magna cum laude. He worked very hard, long hours to achieve that very high honor. When he came back to his Methodist conference in June after graduation, he found that his regional bishop and district superintendent had placed him in a tiny town an hour-and-a-half drive from the nearest town with a book store. That conference starts all their "boys" in places like that. "After all, you have to start somewhere, and it's good to work up through the ranks, like we all did," the district superintendent was heard to say.

Richard doesn't know what to do with himself. The church has 125 members, and he called on all of them the first six months he was there. Very few in the church are interested in Karl Barth (Richard's true love in seminary). When he suggested that the church form a social action committee, they said they had tried that in the sixties and it didn't work—nobody came to the meetings.

Richard is underemployed. He doesn't have a job big enough for his skills. He is serving a church that requires one-third of a minister's time, not three-thirds.

If Richard's situation sounds familiar to you, then read chapter 4.

### Laborsaving Devices

The last chapter of this book is a list of helpful hints, devices, and suggestions for making administration a little more efficient. I have not tried to be complete with my list of ideas. There are numerous books on the market that give long lists of such laborsaving devices that you may find helpful, as I have.[2] The list of ideas that I have here is an inventory of things I use in my own life and ministry. Some will be of use to you, others will not. So pick and choose among them.

**Acknowledgments**

There are a number of people I wish to thank for their considerable efforts on my behalf, helping me to accomplish the writing of this book. First I would like to thank Lyle Schaller whose idea it was that I write a manuscript on time management. He has been very helpful and supportive as the editor of the Creative Leadership Series. Twelve persons, most of them parish clergy, read the the manuscript in draft form and made invaluable suggestions as to how the manuscript might be improved; they are: Lew Towler, Loren Mead, Celia Hahn, Ted Hastings, Reuel Howe, David Swink, Jakie Byers, Tom Schumacher, Tom Kirwan, Jack Byers, Roger Sharp, and Valeta Howe. Carol Cunningham, who works with me as office manager and secretary, has done an excellent job of typing each draft of the manuscript. And to Tom Austin and Margaret Chaney my sincere thanks for input and materials along the way.

Finally, I wish to express very special thanks to Jack Ensroth who has helped me better understand that the way I use my time is not just a function of the amount of work there is to be done. He has helped me see that my time management is also directly related to my hopes, my fears, and my visions of the future.

# I. The Compulsive Worker

> He who does not join in the rejoicing, who does not rest from his work in this joy, despises God's goodness and faithfulness and puts his hope, not in God's election, but in his own work.
>
> Karl Barth, *Church Dogmatics* Vol. III

There are two kinds of poor time management: one is not working enough (underwork), and the other is overwork. The irony is that most of the people who are concerned with "time management" are those who have the latter problem. Often those who want to get more done in less time are already doing more than they should, and the advice they should receive is "do less" rather than "here are fifty-seven ways to do more."

As management consultant to churches, the most common problem I see among clergy is overwork or compulsive work. Overworked pastors are trying to do the best they know how, and the best they know is never to let up. They forget that there is no relation between the amount of time and effort that goes into the minister's work and its effectiveness—none whatsoever. In God's work, rewards are not related to the amount of labor.

> For the kingdom of heaven is like a householder who went out early in the morning to hire laborers for his vineyard. After agreeing with the laborers for a denarius a day, he sent them into his vineyard. And going out about the third hour he saw others standing idle in the market place; and to them he said,

> "You go into the vineyard too, and whatever is right I will give you." So they went. Going out again about the sixth hour and the ninth hour, he did the same. And about the eleventh hour he went out and found others standing; and he said to them, "Why do you stand here idle all day?" They said to him, "Because no one has hired us." He said to them, "You go into the vineyard too." And when evening came, the owner of the vineyard said to his steward, "Call the laborers and pay them their wages, beginning with the last, up to the first." And when those hired about the eleventh hour came, each of them received a denarius. Now when the first came, they thought they would receive more; but each of them also received a denarius. And on receiving it they grumbled at the householder, saying, "These last worked only one hour, and you have made them equal to us who have borne the burden of the day and the scorching heat." But he replied to one of them, "Friend, I am doing you no wrong; did you not agree with me for a denarius? Take what belongs to you, and go; I choose to give to this last as I give to you. Am I not allowed to do what I choose with what belongs to me? So the last will be first, and the first last." (Matt. 20:1-16)

## How Hard Do Clergy Work?

There are studies that give some indication of what an average workweek is for clergy. Three such studies, which seem to corroborate one another, have come to my attention:

1. Samuel Blizzard in a report of the Russell Sage Foundation found 418 local church clergy worked the following hours:

> The professional work day of the cooperating ministers averaged a few minutes less than ten hours. Rural men reported a work day of nine hours and 17 minutes. That of urban ministers was ten hours 32 minutes. Considering all ministerial informants almost two-fifths of their total work day was spent as an administrator. An incidental but revealing item of intelligence is the time parish ministers devote to sermon preparation and to stenographic work each day. The average time devoted to sermon preparation is 34 minutes for rural men, 38 minutes for urban clergymen. The time taken up by stenographic tasks is one hour and four minutes for both country and city men.[1]

2. A 1968 study of 913 clergy of the Episcopal church found the average clergy workweek was 66.7 hours or 11.1 hours a

day for a 6-day week. The Rev. Calhoun W. Wick quoted that study to say that clergy spent their time in the following way:

| | |
|---|---|
| 1. Public worship | 7.5 hours |
| 2. Parish activities, organizations | 37.2 hours |
| 3. Pastoral activities | 15.4 hours |
| 4. Non-church related activities | 3.9 hours |
| 5. Personal prayer and meditation | 2.7 hours |
| | 66.7 hours[2] |

3. Minister's Life did another, more recent study[3] in which they found: "The average work week was 53.7 hours. That's just two hours less than the average week put in by the chief executives of the top 500 U.S. corporations. The average salary of these executives is above $200,000 a year. The average pastoral stipend—about $10,000." (What was that we were saying about the relationship between reward and labor?) The article goes on to identify these hourly averages per week:

| | |
|---|---|
| 1. Meetings and administrative duties | 26.0 hours |
| 2. Hospital and home visitation | 7.0 hours |
| 3. Study and reading | 11.0 hours |
| 4. Personal counseling | 2.2 hours |
| 5. Preparing sermons, funerals and weddings | 7.5 hours |
| | 53.7 hours[3] |

And how much time did they spend with their family? Minister's Life said 6 hours per week! That, I do not believe. If it's true, the clergy who reported to Minister's Life have a lot of time unaccounted for. There are 168 hours in a week, and allowing 8 hours a night for sleep, the above figures leave 52.3 hours per week unaccounted for. Am I to believe that none of those were with family? My guess is that the study asked questions in such a way as to confuse this point, as pastors often do. In fact, all three of the studies are unclear in certain respects. Categories such as "stenographic tasks," "parish activities, organizations," and "meetings and administrative duties" tend to obscure rather than clarify what a pastor does. When medical doctors are engaged in consultation with other doctors about what to do about a particular patient's illness, this could either be desribed as "a meeting" or "diagnostic consultation," "planning," or "part of the therapeutic process." Listing time as merely "meetings" or "phoning" or "administration" usually does not tell the story of what it is that the pastor is trying to accomplish by the activity. I will address this issue again in chapter 3.

What I wish to emphasize here is not so much how the time is spent but the quantity of time spent. The range of hours that a minister works per week was from fifty-four to sixty-seven—in other words, about ten hours per day in a six-day week. Therefore, half of all clergy work more than ten hours per day, and that, to my mind, is strong evidence that one of the severe personal problems of clergy today is compulsive working.

We have some other evidence for this. Less than a year ago, I did a study of the leisure activities of clergy for the Institute for Advanced Pastoral Studies.[4] One of the findings in that study was that compared with a control group of residents in Marin County, California, clergy in my sample showed significantly less interest in a category of recreational activities called "slow living." This category included the following: dining out, driving/motoring, exercising, gardening, going to movies, listening to the radio, listening to records, reading (books, plays, poetry, newspapers/ magazines), sightseeing, talking on the telephone, visiting friends, visiting museums, window-shopping, and writing letters.

From earlier studies that were done of the personality types of people who scored low in this slow-living category (such as the clergy in my study), it was learned by George McKechnie that they tended to have personality characteristics of self-control, order, and concern for their own adequacy as persons. They do not feel they can afford to sit back and take their ease from time to time; rather, they are overly concerned with their adequacy as persons and deny themselves the everyday indulgences of these slow-living activities. To quote from the original study:

> People who lead full, active, perhaps hectic lives, who are heavily involved in their career of family-raising, from time to time need a change of pace, a chance to slow down, and relax. This is what slow living is all about. For these people, the slow paced activity of watching TV, window shopping, or talking with friends on the telephone are a refreshing respite and well-earned reward.
>
> Persons scoring high on this cluster are planful, efficient, energetic individuals who work hard and play easy. They indulge themselves in the simple but satisfying everyday pleasures that allow for relaxation and the expression of complete autonomy.[5]

Clergy and others who score low, on the other hand, indicate a tendency toward professional self-doubt and the high probability of a need to overcompensate for this uncertainty by denying themselves the simple pleasures of time off to relax and indulge in leisure activities.

**What Are the Marks of a Compulsive Worker?**

Here is my checklist of items that may indicate that you are working too much, and are becoming (or have become compulsive about work:)

1. You work more than sixty hours per week.
2. You brag to others about how many hours per day or days per week you are working.
3. You can't think of anything to talk about at a party other than your work.
4. You are unable to say no to any individual or committee that asks you to do something.
5. Your spouse asks if you have given up him or her for Lent.
6. You feel depressed much of the time.
7. When you go on a vacation, you take more than one book for each day you will be away.

8. You set goals for yourself that are unrealistic and unattainable.
9. Your daughter asks if she can make an appointment to talk with you.
10. You are noticing increasing rigidity in yourself to new concepts and programs, an inflexibility that says no to change.
11. You find fault with everyone and everything around, complaining about the church and reacting cynically to whatever is attempted or suggested by others.
12. You have more than two books on time management in your library.
13. Your first impulse is to work harder as a way to solve problems rather than to use Fuch's dictim: "Think. Maybe we can dodge some work."

**Why Are Clergy and Others Compulsive Workers?**

Michael Kinsley calls the compulsive working of the people in the Carter administration "time macho."[6] Time macho, as Kinsley describes it, is the attempt of the compulsive to prove his or her worth and power through certain rituals and activities that are used to ward off the fears and uncertainties that pervade life. The hope is that by working harder, by putting in long hours, and by intently focusing on that work you will at least get an *A* for effort, even if you are not able to reach your grandiose goals. Both elements are there in the time-macho person: the need to accomplish more than anyone else in the block (or, in history for some) and the need to keep at it, never to let up, as if you were Peter, the little Dutch boy, with your finger in the dike. Should you leave, the whole thing will collapse. These two needs come from the same sources of uncertainty or fear and take on several different manifestations. Let's look at some of them.

*Fear of Death.* Wayne Oates talks powerfully about fear of death when he writes:

> The early Christians celebrated a "day of rest and gladness" once a week on "the first day of the week." They did so as a reminder that their Lord was resurrected on that day. To them

> the bondage from which they were set free was the fear of death itself. This fear is the master fear which prompts the workaholic to work compulsively. I have never met a work addict that I did not think was preoccupied subconsciously with the imminence of his own death. He works intensely, as if there is only a very little time left in which to accomplish his tasks. He runs the race of life as if the Grim Reaper were just behind him, gaining on him and aiming to cut him down all of a sudden.
>
> Death is the symbol of ultimate impotence and finiteness to the workaholic. Work, on the other hand, assuages the feeling of impotence and demonstrates competence. It is to the work addict what sex is to the philanderer. The accomplishment of more and more work temporarily wards off the anxiety of death. However, when the weekend comes, and the defense of work is no longer available, the "Lord's Day" is a reminder of death and not a celebration of the renewal of life through resurrection.[7]

Joyce Brothers says that a compulsive worker is driven by "a terror that if you give it up, if you stop the ritual, something terrible will happen." Most of us are not fully conscious of this fear. We do not go around thinking out loud to ourselves, "If I don't work hard, something terrible will happen." But those fears and fantasies capture us from time to time and reveal the truth beneath them: Why do you hide the flyfisherman's magazine when you hear your wife coming near the study door? Why are you uncomfortable playing tennis on your day off on the courts two blocks from the church? Why do you get depressed before going on or during a vacation? These are probably clues that we are

> trying extra hard to protect [ourselves] against the accidents of life and danger of death . . . trying to pass [ourselves] off as anything but an animal. . . . These behavior patterns are a 'fabricated' protest against natural reality, a denial of the truth of the human condition, and an attempt to forget the pathetic creature that man is.[8]

*Fear of Failure.* Less general, but just as real, are those specific fears that each of us has that we will not be successful. Do you remember in seminary when you were studying for an exam or preparing to write a term paper? You were never quite certain that you had read enough, that you had studied all the sources, that you were adequately prepared. So, if you were a compulsive worker, you set almost no limits to your work and tried to fill yourself with all knowledge in order to not fail.

There is a kind of irrational thinking that goes on in the mind of the compulsive worker who is afraid of failure. The ministry is an environment in which it can easily happen. It is very difficult to measure the results of one's work in this profession. We work with people in rather nonstructured situations where formal evaluation is infrequent and informal evaluation almost never direct. Therefore, it is very hard to know how you're doing because you can't measure your products, and you don't get much clear feedback. If you can't measure output, you measure input. And in order to convince yourself that you're doing a "good" job, you count the large number of hours and the large amount of energy and the large amount of anxiety you put into the job. It may not be the best measure, you say to yourself, but it's better than nothing.

*Fear of Intimacy.* Another possible root of compulsive behavior is fear of intimacy. Hard work is a wonderful way to avoid getting close to people and taking the risks of close personal relationships. Work can be the shield that protects you from spending "too much" time with your family. It can be an excuse to refer to other professionals most of the people who come in to see you for counseling. It can also be a cover to make it difficult for you to find time to do your calling.

Compulsive workers have a very clear but subtle way of putting others off. They let it be known by a glance at the watch, little comments to hurry the conversation along, or their tense and strained posture that they just don't have time for you. The root of this may be their fear of death or failure. If they "wasted" time with one person, they won't be able to do all the other things that are necessary for "success"; or it may very well be a fear of what might happen when you get close to another person.

*Fear of Being Alone with Yourself.* Another fear that may exist in the life of the compulsive is a fear of silence and/or being alone in unstructured time. One person said to me, "I'd rather be working than thinking," as he was describing the hour each day he spent in his car commuting to his place of employment. Here was a gift of two hours a day this man had to be with just himself, to be open to the working of the Holy Spirit in his inner life. Not only was the time an opportunity for inner exploration, it was socially acceptable. No one would ask any questions about the time "wasted" in commuting as someone might had the word gotten out that he spent two hours each morning in meditative silence. Because of his fear of himself, my friend in order to cope with the silence, bought a tape recorder and now uses the two hours every day to do his dictation, to listen to tapes on profound subjects, and to learn Morse code and Spanish.

*Seeking Recognition.* Another feature of compulsive work is that it is a wonderful means for playing "mine is bigger than yours," a childish game that some have not outgrown. Michael Kinsley took on James Reston for playing the game with these words:

> James Reston interrupted one of his recent Washington weather reports . . . to observe that Secretary of State Cyrus Vance "is putting in so many hours that he's scarcely getting the minimum wage." Reston probably thought this was pretty cute, but it demonstrated once again how far out of touch he and other Washington movers and shakers are from the life around them.
>
> To earn his annual salary of $63,000 at the federal minimum wage of $2.30 per hour, Vance would have to work 75 hours a day, 365 days a year. This doesn't include federal employee perks such as health care and pension benefits. Nor does it reflect the fact that Secretary Vance, unlike his fellow minimum wage workers in the private sector, needn't contribute to social security. Working a more reasonable 24 hours a day every day for a year, Vance would earn $20,148 or with time and a half for overtime, $27,830. The $63,000 is not a lavish amount for Vance's job, but it bears no serious comparison to the minimum wage.[9]

We clergy use the same hyperbole as Mr. Reston, especially when it comes to talking about how hard we work.

Whether I am in a clergy conference or listening to a pastor give a report to the session on last month's work, to hear pastors tell it you would think they were the most oppressed class on earth. I suppose a good deal of this is compensatory since they cannot measure their worth to society in terms of tangible products or salary. They therefore try to measure their worth in terms of the intensity and length of their work.

*Injunctions and Prescriptions.* In Transactional Analysis, Eric Berne talks about another root of compulsive behavior that may also be one of its causes.[10] Injunctions are prohibitions learned from one's parents that are reinforced through repetition/approval ("You've been nice and quiet") or discouragement ("Don't be too ambitious"). Prescriptions are encouragements that are meant to bring the person to well-being and success: "Save your money," "Don't eat starches," or "Never sit on a public toilet seat." There are many injunctions and prescriptions that people have learned as children that they may still believe will get them out of stress or difficulty. They believe that if they follow these "rules," things will get better. Here are some that are directly relevant: "Try hard, "Please others," "Hurry up," "Be strong," "Be perfect."

Usually these "rules" don't work. They are supposed to get you going, but they do the opposite. They become blocks to your ability to increase your effectiveness and your efficiency. Trying hard is the worst thing you can do if you're attempting to hit a baseball. Tensing your muscles and overconcentrating make your movements awkward and ineffective. If you try to please others as your first rule of life, you don't please yourself, and you will learn the hard way that often you can't please others anyway. "Hurry up!" leads to mistakes. It makes you and everyone else nervous. Speed reading is a good example of this. Reading in a hurry not only takes away the pleasure, it significantly reduces the learning.

## Costs of Compulsive Work

The reason that there are laws against long-distance truckers' driving more than eight hours and against airline pilots flying more than a set number of hours at a time is that tired people make mistakes. Mistakes by truck drivers and airline pilots can be fatal. For those who must excel at their profession, being tired or worn out is too costly a price to pay. Excellence does not come from tired people, mediocrity does. Professional athletes, musicians, surgeons, and others whose work demands excellence, build time into their schedules for rest, leisure, and diversion so that they will have the highest quality instrument (themselves) with which to work.

In addition to doing mediocre work, workaholics have a lower quality relationship with others. They are irritable, bored, fussy, and distant. It is hard to get close to them. If one does get close, it is only for a short time. Work compulsives are to time what Scrooge was to money: They are so busy trying to save it and protect it that they throw out the baby of life with the bath water of indolence.

Further, those whose noses are always to the grindstone, lose their creativity, their ability to come up with new ideas and fresh solutions to problems. In almost all the literature on creativity, there is some mention made of the importance of play and rest as necessary ingredients in problem-solving. Some believe that there is a censor that functions to protect the conscious mind from interrupting unconscious thoughts.[11] New ideas do not come from the rational or conscious part of the mind. They come from the subconsious. (Some would say from the right side of the brain.) When one is in a state of intention to so solve a problem, when one is really trying to figure something out, it is the left side of the brain that is at work, and the ideas from the right side are prohibited from the conscious mind by the censor. In order to get at all of one's knowledge, a person has to do the opposite of what seems right to do. Instead of thinking harder, one has to back off, to think less, to do something else in order to let the subconscious resources break through.

I have always been impressed by the creative process desribed in Watson's book *The Double Helix*. Watson (along with Crick) discovered the structure of DNA molecules. He explains that his work on the problem of the molecule's structure included a great deal of nonwork time away from the lab. He loved to have lingering meals at lunch and dinner. He enjoyed teatime and rarely missed it; he certainly would not miss a party where young ladies would be present; movies were a regular part of his evening life. His remembrance of his days during the era when he was working on DNA is full of references to his leisure-time:

> The next few days saw Francis becoming increasingly agitated by my failure to stick close to the molecular models. It did not matter that before his tenish entrance I was usually in the lab. Almost every afternoon, knowing that I was on the tennis court, he would fretfully twist his head away from his work to see the polynucleotide backbone unattended. Moreover, after tea I would show up for only a few minutes of fiddling before dashing away to have sherry with the girls at Pop's. . . . I went ahead spending most evenings at the films, vaguely dreaming that any moment the answer would suddenly hit me.[12]

Another description shows that Watson was aware that it was necessary for ideas to incubate and for his subconscious store of information to percolate to the surface without undue pressure. Whether this incubation is in the presence of the trappings of science, in the laboratory, or at tea or tennis did not seem to be relevant. What is relevant is the pace or style at which one approaches the problems with which one is dealing. Even after they were close to a solution of the problem of the shape of the molecule, Watson writes:

> The following morning I felt marvelously alive when I awoke. On my way to the Whim I **slowly walked** toward the Clare Bridge, staring up at the gothic pinnacles of the King's College Chapel that stood out sharply against the spring sky. I **briefly stopped** and looked over at the perfect Georgian features of the recently cleaned Gibbs Building, thinking that much of our success was due to the long **uneventful periods** when we walked among the colleges or unobstrusively read the new books that come into Heffer's Bookstore. After **contentedly pouring** over *The Times,* I wandered into the lab to see Francis, unquestionably early, flipping the cardboard base pairs about the imaginary line.[13] (Emphasis added)

This need to back off and relax in order to find creativity is corroborated by Prince:

> Each of us has come to depend upon one technique or another for getting new ideas. Usually we have arrived at a procedure almost unconsciously by trial and error. A key element in such procedures is the mulling over, sometimes called incubation. This point may come early or after much work, when one seems to have gone as far as he can and is still without a new viewpoint. He temporarily puts the problem out of his mind and takes a vacation from it. This is a matter of degree; some people seem to completely forget the problem, while others temporarily turn their attention to something else. People take this vacation from the problem with some assurance that a clue will come to them. It usually does while shaving, bathing, cutting the grass, driving a familiar route to work, waking from sleep, or going to sleep. Each person seems to have a favorite time or activity. In each case the censor is lulled to inattention, and the valuable raw material is slipped past it.
>
> In addition to the famous example of history (Archimedes and Eureka!, Poincaré descending from the bus, etc.), many people have told us of such experiences. A minister told of his long-time worry over boring his congregation. As he was shaving one morning the thought popped into his consciousness: "Hire theater critics." He felt excited about his thought but did not immediately understand either the thought's significance or his excitement. Puzzling, he suddenly realized this was a way of improving his sermons. He appointed representative observers to give him their reactions after each sermon. His reviews started out poor, but pace and sharpness improved and his congregation increased.[14]

Finally, those who are stuck working all the time lose what Eric Berne calls autonomy. Autonomy is manifested by the release or recovery of three capacities: awareness, spontaneity, and intimacy. He contemptuously calls a person without awareness a Jerk:

> The man whose chief preoccupation is being on time is the one who is furthest out. With his body at the wheel of his car, his mind is at the door of his office. And he is oblivious to his immediate surroundings except insofar as they are obstacles to

> the moment when his soma will catch up with his psyche. This is the Jerk, whose chief concern is how it will look to the boss. If he is late, he will take pains to arrive out of breath. The compliant Child is in command, and his game is "Look How Hard I've Tried." While he is driving, he is almost completely lacking in autonomy, and as a human being he is in essence more dead than alive. It is quite possible that this is the most favorable condition for the development of hypertension or coronary disease.[15]

One can also describe awareness positively, as did Marya Mannes in her poem "Time, Gentlemen, Please":

> Lie down and listen to the crabgrass grow,
> The faucet leak, and learn to leave them so.
> Feel how the breezes play about your hair
> And sunlight settles on your breathing skin.
> What else can matter but the drifting glance
> On dragonfly or sudden shadow there
> Of swans aloft and the whiffle of their wings
> On air to other ponds? Nothing but this:
> To see, to wonder, to receive, to feel
> What lies in the circle of your singleness.
> Think idly of a woman or a verse
> Or bees or vapor trails or why the birds
> Are still at noon. Yourself, be still—
> There is no living when you're nagging time
> And stunting every second with your will.
> You work for this: to be the sovereign
> Of what you slave to have—not
> Slave.

**What to Do About Compulsive Working**

The most significant thing that you can do about compulsive working is to deal with the fears that you are trying to assuage through this behavior. Many find it helpful to get professional help in doing this. Especially if your compulsive working has reached a crisis stage, counseling can help you cope with your problems, and it certainly is better to consult a psychologist or psychiatrist or psychotherapist before your spouse leaves, your ministry deteriorates, or other disasters emerge.

However, you may want to try some things on your own to

see if you can redirect your course before it reaches crisis proportions. The following ideas I have found to be helpful to clergy in my time management classes and in my own life.

*Be Compulsive About Rest.* Those of us who are compulsive about work are probably compulsive about a lot of things. We are overly concerned and compelled to do something about the messiness of life. We are trying to keep everything in order and everything in its place. We don't like dirt, we don't like confusion, we don't like laziness, we don't like waste. If we have strong urges to get control of these foibles, it is possible for us to use these drives for our own betterment rather than let them take us into further difficulty.

In my own life, I have found it helpful to be rigid about my scheduling; so I plan for breaks, rest, play, and fun. Admittedly, this is second best to being able to enjoy the moment and live good times as they happen. However, I have a bad case of a need for order, planfulness, and work. Here are some of the ways that I make time for those needs I repress and often consciously do not recognize:

I incorporate days off into my schedule a year in advance. I figure the amount of time that I think I should take off in a year and then design my year so that rest and recreation are in every week of my schedule. Each week has days marked on my calendar with *R & R.* These days are just as rigidly protected as those days that say "Meet with my conference minister to discuss my next job." If something very important comes up so that I cannot take off on my R & R day, I take another day that week or I write in another R & R day in the next week, or two weeks hence.

I also do lots of counting. I count my days off, I count the days I work at writing, the days spent with clients, the days spent in preparation for work. All this counting reassures my compulsive self that I have earned my time off and I don't have to feel guilty about it. The fact is that one's leisure does not have to be won. It is as much a part of life and growth as is work. To assume that work is morally superior is inaccurate. As Robert Lee says:

> Since all of life must be regarded as a whole, it is artificial to compartmentalize leisure time from work or from the rest of time. . . . Leisure is the growing time of the human spirit. . . .
>
> Those who seek to define leisure in opposition to work fail to account sufficiently for the interpenetration of work and leisure, for the many ways in which work and play are suffused. Their views imply that leisure is a reward for sweat—something that must be earned through productive effort, much as a beast of burden deserves food and a night's rest as a reward for the day's toil. Leisure need not be viewed as subordinate to work or as a restorative for work, but may be seen as an end in itself, something valued for its own sake.[16]

Nonetheless, there are some of us who still have not been able to make the differentiation and who in our heart of hearts believe that somehow our first and most important calling is to our profession and that family, God, and our own private lives can be significantly subordinated to our vocation. Those of us who find it difficult to believe in the value of rest are the ones who have to count. It is hoped that we will grow out of this need for a crutch or this unbelief or faithlessness, but for the time being we will have to use this device.

Use your calendar to decide how many days or hours should be spent in professional work, how many in leisure, how many with other pursuits you feel are appropriate in your life. Put the days or hours in your calendar, *in ink,* and then when they have to be changed, add replacements as you go along.

*Join Something.* Another way to help pull you away from your tendency to be consumed by your work is to get involved with others in an activity that is separate from your work life. Joining can have a number of helpful reinforcing properties. If others are depending on you to hold up your end of a bargain, this commitment will be a spur to goad you from your work. When I was in graduate school I had an appointment every Tuesday afternoon with a friend to play handball. He was always at the court at that time. If I didn't show up, I knew he would be annoyed. Our agreement helped us both take a much needed break from the books.

Joining with others who are not members of your church can help in developing personal relationships that are not dependent on the structure of a job to hold them up. You can get involved with people for their own interest to you, without any utility as far as your profession or career is concerned. We have friends who belong to a gourmet cooking club. Once a month they go to the home of a different person who prepares a specialty meal for the rest of the group. In this setting they are able to develop close personal relationships, admire one another's food and homes, and enjoy the renewal that comes from a nonutilitarian use of time.

Joining a group of persons who are interested in the same non–work-related subjects can provide stimulus for deeper exploration than might come from a hobby engaged in alone. If you are interested in photography or radio transmitting or lapidary or horology or gardening or skiing or whatever, your knowledge and enjoyment can be enhanced by being with others who are also exploring the same pursuits. Some of these hobbies require so much technical information to get started that you might be discouraged before you get into them enough to find them rewarding. To join with others helps you learn quickly, gets you directed to things that you can get satisfaction from early in the process, and gives you ideas about the exciting possibilities these pursuits could have in your future.

If you are finding it difficult to stick with a leisure pursuit after you have begun, as a last resort, may I suggest that you invest money in your project, and not just a token amount; invest enough to show that you are seriously committed to the idea. If you are not sticking to an exercise regime each day or each week because "more important" things are getting in the way, pay Vic Tanny or Jack La Lanne or your local YMCA for the privilege of exercising in their facility. The investment often will nag at you and pull you back to what you should have been doing if you lag behind. I have also found it helpful in my own experience to pay for correspondence courses on nonwork subjects that are of interest to me. You can take such courses on almost any subject you can imagine: photography, art, radio repair, watch repair, gardening, car repair, fly-tying, locksmithing, literature, and so on. Many such courses are quite reasonable in cost through public colleges and universities. If you are interested in a particular subject and want to see what courses are available, go to a magazine that specializes in the subject, and you will find ads for places that offer such courses.

*Introspection.* Looking inward is another way to begin to deal with your compulsive work habits. It may be that the roots of your behavior come from one or more of the fears mentioned in the beginning of this chapter. Some have found it helpful to try to list these fears. Sit down with a piece of paper and head it: What Am I Afraid Of? Now list anything that comes to mind. Once you have a nice long list, examine it and ask yourself the question: Which of these fears is likely to come to pass? Those that seem to be particularly "ripe" are good candidates for further exploration. Write fantasy scenarios about them. What would it be like if the worst thing that could happen happened? Envision yourself completely messing up, doing everything wrong. What would that be like? Now, write another scenario envisioning yourself doing everything well and adequately.

For example, one pastor wrote a scenario about his fear of losing his family because of his compulsive work habits. He envisioned his wife having an affair with another man, his children rejecting him, his children not knowing what his views and concerns about life are; he envisioned himself lonely and forsaken. Once this was completed he wrote a fantasy of a perfect week that would include time for his wife and children. He noted a certain number of free evenings, he noted a ball game with the boys, he noted the quality of dinner-time conversation, and he noted a "date" once a week with his wife. After he had written this fantasy he listed several policies that he could now incorporate in his life that would get him what he wanted in terms of quality time with his family. One of the policies had to do with taking more time off. Another had to do with taking fifteen minutes with each child alone during the day; another had to do with spending less time on sermon preparation and finishing his sermon by Friday so he would not be preoccupied with it on Saturday evening.

*Ask for help from friends.* Another technique you can use is asking a trusted friend to help you with your "problem." Make a regular appointment with another pastor or individual who can help you reflect on your intentions to be less compulsive about your work. Some have found that their secretary can help with this. It is a good idea to agree with your helper to meet for at least a year in this process and check with each other at least once a month. Shorter time than that will not give the desired results.

In the first conversations identify what you want to stop doing and what you want to start doing. Don't be in a hurry to decide everything once and for all. Start small, with, for example, the issue of time spent in sermon preparation. If you decide to spend no more than ten hours per week on this, then talk about which hours would be best, where is the best place to work (at home or the office or the library), how far in advance to prepare topics, and so on. Write down your agreements. Then, observe yourself as you go through the next month. Keep track of the times you do well and the times that you do poorly on your new resolve. What happened that caused things to go awry? What helped? Do you need more policies? less? As you begin to get sermon preparation under satisfactory control, then move on to other areas of concern in your life: time with your family, your private devotion-time, the amount of time you spend in exercise and keeping your body fit, and so on.

*Meditation.* Finally, I recommend that you set up several times each day when you stop doing everything. If you need justification from a physical point of view as to why that is helpful, read Herbert Benson's book *The Relaxation Response.*[17] If you need theological justification for it, read Douglas Steere's *On Beginning from Within/On Listening to Another,* or Henri Nouwen's *Reaching Out,* or Edgar Jackson's *Understanding Prayer.* You will find that taking short breaks from time to time will help you relax, not take yourself and your activity so seriously, and give you a new focus and energy.

It is important that you do not take large chunks of time to start. If you do, you will quickly tire of the process and find it irksome. Instead, take two- to five-minute breaks for spiritual refreshment three or four times per day. The results will greatly surprise you.

Here is the process that Benson recommends:

> There appear to be four basic elements underlying the elicitation of the Relaxation Response, regardless of the cultural source.
>
> The first element is a *quiet environment.* One must "turn off" not only internal stimuli but also external distractions. A quiet room or a place of worship may be suitable. The nature mystics meditated outdoors.
>
> The second element is an *object to dwell upon.* This object may be a word or sound repetition of a syllable will help clear the mind. When distracting thoughts do occur, one can return to this repetition of the syllable to help eliminate other thoughts.
>
> The third element is a *passive attitude.* It is an emptying of all thoughts and distractions from one's mind. *A passive attitude appears to be the most essential factor in eliciting the Relaxation Response.* Thought, imagery, and feeling may drift into one's awareness. One should not concentrate on these perceptions but allow them to pass on. A person should not be concerned with how well he or she is doing.
>
> The fourth element is a *comfortable position.* One should be in a comfortable posture that will allow an individual to remain in the same position for at least twenty minutes. Usually a sitting position is recommended. We believe the sitting, kneeling, squatting, swaying postures assumed in various forms of prayer have evolved to keep the practitioner from falling asleep. The desired altered state of consciousness is not sleep, but the same four elements will lead to sleep if the practitioner is lying down.[18]

Compulsive behavior is not easily dealt with, and you should not assume that these ideas of being compulsive about rest, joining something, introspection, asking for help and meditation will make it all go away. In fact, the risk here is that the compulsive will choose to be rigid in his or her approach to not being compulsive, thus defeating the good intentions. Perhaps the next time you find yourself all caught up in anxious business, trying to solve everybody else's problems and guarantee your own success, you might think of the saying that has been attributed to the Buddha by some of the Eastern mystics: "Don't just do something, sit there."

# II. The Procrastinator

Procrastination is the thief of time;
Year after year it steals, till all are fled,
And to the mercy of a moment leaves
The vast concerns of an eternal scene.

Edward Young, *Night Thoughts I*

There are, unless my memory fail,
Five causes why we should not sail:
The fog is thick, the wind is high;
It rains; or may do, by and by;
Or any other reason why.

Frederick C. Gill,
*In the Steps of John Wesley*

The word *procrastinate* has interesting roots. The prefix *pro* comes from the Latin that means "forward" or "in front of," and you see it used in the words *proceed,* which means to go forward (*cede:* "to go"), and *progress,* which means to walk or step forward (*gradi:* "to step"), and *project,* which means to cast or throw forward *(jacere:* "to throw"). *Cras* in Latin means "tomorrow"; hence; to procrastinate is to put forward until tomorrow. In the early history of the word it does not seem to have had necessarily negative connotations, but its general usage today is "to put off or delay *without justification."*

Three methods of procrastination are common in the ministry. The first occurs when one postpones a particular task until it is too late to do anything about it. A good idea for a Fourth of July pageant on which no action was taken until the middle of June is one of those things that died for lack of attention. Calling on people who were in church for the first time last Sunday can be delayed too long—until they join another congregation.

Getting the work done late is another aspect of procrastination. The pledge campaign that was supposed to have started in October but actually started on the Sunday before Thanksgiving is an illustration of procrastination. The Christian Education Curriculum was not ordered in the summer so you started the fall program without resources in the Sunday school is another.

These two common methods of procrastination, while commonly known to us, are not as frequent as the third which is frantic activity undertaken at the last minute to beat the deadline. Those Saturday night sermon-writing sessions are an example of this. On several occasions in my first parish, I found myself in the church office on Saturday typing and running off the bulletin on the mimeograph machine because I didn't have the material ready for it in time for my secretary to do her job.

There are eight frequent causes of procrastination in the ministry. In this chapter I discuss the causes and suggest some things that you might do to correct each difficulty.

### You Don't Understand the Problem

Quite often the reason we put off doing a job is that we don't fully understand what's happening. If we could just have a little more certainty about the issue, if we just felt a little more secure about what is needed or what is going on, then we would do something to rectify the situation.

Not long ago I was working with a congregation that was having difficulty with a drop in church school attendance. At the meetings of the Christian Education Committee over several months, the members would make tentative suggestions as to the reasons for the decline. One night they discussed the fact that member families had fewer children than families in the past. A month later they discussed the perceived decrease in quality of the curriculum from their denominational publishing house, and on the third month they took on the teachers as being poorly trained and not committed to their work. Each time they raised the subject of the shrinking school, the Christian Education Committee members knew that they were talking off the top of their heads and had not done any research to confirm their hunches or focus their efforts. Therefore, at each meeting, ideas were suggested, but commitment was lacking to invest any time or energy or money to improve the situation.

What that committee and I did after several months of discomfort was to develop a process to find out what the problem or problems were and then to select certain specific problems to work on. Our first task, then, was to define the problem. What was needed was a clear problem-definition that everyone understood and to which it was easy to address ourselves. The clear problem-definition made it possible for us to get started easily and took away our need to postpone any action because of our uncertainty.

After we had gathered a good deal of information from the teachers, children, and parents who were in the Sunday school and from those who were members of the church not attending the church school, two very clear facts emerged. One was that there was a severe discipline problem in the church school classes themselves, and the other was that teachers did little to prepare lesson plans or structured activities for the children. Once these problems were identified, the Christian Education Committee was able to commit itself to finding the resources needed to deal with the problems they saw before them. What they did was ask the denomination to send their regional Christian education staff person to their church for four consecutive Saturdays to train their teachers in how to use the denomination's curriculum and how to manage discipline problems on Sunday morning. The improvements in attendance and attitude were almost immediately apparent to everyone.

## You Are Unable to Decide

Another common cause of procrastination is your inability to make up your mind. Some people equate procrastination with this cause. Certainly it is a common cause. If you could decide what you wanted to do, you would do it. But because there is some uncertainty or because all the alternatives seem equally bad or all the alternatives seem equally good, you tend to hold back and wait until some revelation comes that will help you get on with it.

Two years ago, my old car was finding it more and more difficult to get going in the morning. The tires were wearing out, it was drinking oil as if it were trying to fund the Alaska pipeline, and the upholstery was hanging down on the back of my head when the wind didn't blow it toward the back of the car. But it was paid for. It seemed better to put dribbles of money into it than to make a regular monthly payment for a newer vehicle. Procrastination seemed to be the order of the day. I could wait until the old car died—and then I would get an even smaller trade-in—or I could wait until I had a down payment for a new car—but the old one might not make it, or it might eat up the cash I was trying to save for another—or I could invest in fixing up the old model.

In the ministry, one often comes up against similar issues on which it is difficult to make a decision. Shall I submit my dossier to other congregations for a possible move to another church? Should the church begin a fund-raising campaign to refurbish the sanctuary? Has the church reached the size that we should hire a director of religious education? And so on.

In order to deal with the procrastination that comes from inability to make decisions, you need to know that the two most important dimensions of decision-making are objective and subjective. Most of the literature in the management field addresses itself to the objective decision-making process. That is, it focuses on "the problem-solving process" which has been quoted and requoted in the literature. Here is Gordon Lippit's rendition of this process:

> **Defining the Problem.** Exploring, clarifying, refining, and rationalizing the problem so that it becomes a group property and, ideally, so that each member is committed to doing something about it.

**Collecting Ideas.** Gathering a wide range of ideas and possibilities, including very tentative alternatives and solutions. Post one evaluation or testing of these ideas. Immediate evaluation of one idea tends to inhibit production of new ideas—for while an idea may seem silly or ridiculous, it may actually be only different and new.

**Testing Ideas and Developing Alternatives.** Assembling information, opinions, and data which may be necessary for evaluating ideas; looking at alternatives, estimating consequences of various actions (predicting what will happen rather than outright criticism), and reality testing.

**Deciding.** In view of previous considerations, choosing the most desirable action, determining who makes the decision and what procedure is followed.[1]

The subjective dimensions of problem-solving, however, must also be taken fully into consideration. As anyone knows, just getting the facts is inadequate for making a decision. Internally a person must assent to the facts, agree to a commitment, and feel confident about the choice. Choice or decision without confidence is not likely to be a firm decision, and procrastination will continue. Meditation and prayer are very important resources in this regard. The key in meditation of this kind is listening or observing; it is being aware of what is going on inside yourself. Telling God your problems and asking for help are important and valuable, but you have to stop telling and asking long enough to hear the answers when they come. Therefore, nothing can be more valuable than silence. Counting each time you exhale while sitting in silence can be helpful in clearing the mind so that one is open to mental messages that are there. Some people find it helpful to use a mantra, or phrase, along with their breathing to clear the mind of other thoughts. Some use "Come Lord Jesus"; others "Lord Have Mercy"; others use favorite texts or phrases that have meaning to them. In other words, by putting aside the problem about which you are to make a decision, you may hear an answer without addressing it directly.

Other meditation devices I have found helpful in decision-making are these:

Spend fifteen minutes a day in silent, nondirected meditation. After the silent meditation, write in a log or journal those thoughts that come to you. Don't try to write a story or complete ideas; just jot down what goes through your mind. As you read back over this material and keep track of it for a time, you may find new ideas and commitments emerging.

In your meditation, have a dialogue with Christ about the problem you are dealing with. Some like to write out the dialogue; others simply let it flow in their head. Let Christ speak as he will, and let your own fantasies and thoughts take you where they will. You may become aware of messages about what you want and what God wants for you.

Another meditation technique is to remember everything you have ever said or done in a situation like this one. When did you make a decision that you liked? When did you make one that did not turn out so well? What were the qualities of the good decision? What were the qualities of a poor decision? Now fantasize about all going well in this decision. What will be its marks? Does this give you any ideas about what you want to do now?

Finally, you can dialogue in your imagination with the problem or persons in the decision itself. Talk to them. Ask them what they would do. Listen to their answers, and be aware of your own responses. Trust those attractions and repulsions that you have within yourself. They will give you important clues as to your own desires and commitments.

**Forgetting**

Forgetting is another form of procrastination. Freud, you will recall, talks about forgetting in his writing.[2] While in many instances he draws conclusions that seem to me to be stretching or overstating the point, in general I find his arguments convincing. He says that forgetting "in all cases is proved to be founded on a motive of displeasure." From his experience he concluded that there is operative in all of us what he called a "counterwill" which is interference in the remembering processes from unknown or unadmitted motives. Sometimes we forget because of an antagonism to conventional duty, or antagonism toward a particular person, or toward the job itself, or any of a hundred other sources of pain or displeasure. To illustrate this point, Freud uses this example:

> A lover who is late at the appointed place will vainly tell his sweetheart that unfortunately he has entirely forgotten their rendezvous. She will not hesitate to answer him: "A year ago you would not have forgotten. Evidently you no longer care for me." Even if he should grasp the cited psychologic explanation, and should wish to excuse his forgetting on the plea of important business, he would only elicit the answer from the woman, who has become as keensighted as the physician in the psychoanalytic treatment, "How remarkable that such business disturbances did not occur before!" Of course the woman does not wish to deny the possibility of forgetting; but she believes, and not without reason, that practically the same inference of a certain unwillingness may be drawn from the unintentional forgetting as from a conscious subterfuge.[3]

If you have trouble remembering appointments, jobs that need to be done in the church, or remembering to pick up your daughter from nursery school, your counterwill is probably at work. This is not to say that the forgetting is intentional in the sense that it is a consciously willed deceit. What it reveals is that below your conscious intentions, you have other wishes and feelings that may not be immediately known to you.

The best way to deal with forgetting, then, is to try to find out just what it is that is creating your resistance to doing what you consciously intend. Sometimes this can be done with a little introspection; you can say to yourself: "Why did I forget that? What is there about doing that which is unpleasant to me? Am I afraid of something here? Am I trying to punish someone? Am I trying to punish myself?"

If individual introspection leaves you baffled, try talking it over with a friend. Indicate to him or her the pattern of forgetting that seems to be occurring, and ask for speculations, along with yours, as to the cause.

Of course, you will never exclude your counterwill from your life, and forgetting is going to occur from time to time. Therefore, it is advisable to keep lists of everything that you have to do. Both important and not-so-important items should be kept track of. Many people update these lists daily; they should be updated at least weekly to assess what has been done, what needs to be done, and to give some thought as to when the work will get done. See the section in chapter 5 on lists for more detail on the different ways to make lists.

### Working Under Pressure

Some people have said to me; "The reason I procrastinate is that I work best under pressure. I put off things to the last minute purposefully." To my mind this is a rationalization. There is some evidence that shows that people work harder under the stress of conflict and deadlines, but there is no evidence that says they work better.

There are many reasons to avoid this kind of procrastination. In the church, and for that matter in any voluntary organization, most of the work is done by cooperation and collaboration in a committee. Participatory management is the best kind of management for that kind of organization. Groups that work under stress, research has shown, usually give up their participatory style and move to hierarchical forms of leadership under the pressure of time. A predilection for working under pressure may be an attempt to either work alone or get control.

Further, last-minute hurry ups are not appreciated by others who have to coordinate themselves to accommodate this rationalization. It is unfair and unnecessary to put your secretary regularly under the gun of your need for pressure in order to get work out.

Working under a short, immediate deadline also gives you no room for dealing with unexpected problems. What if the mimeo machine breaks down or you discover a whole new area that needs exploration before you can make the final decision? Waiting until the last minute gives you no opportunity to take care of these difficulties.

Finally, working under last-minute deadlines may be a convenient cover you use to avoid taking full responsibility for sloppy or incomplete work. It may seem to mitigate or excuse the burden of a poor product if you can say, "Well, the sermon may not have really been up to what it should have been because I wrote it last night." It is a lame excuse, the need for which could have been completely avoided had you set deadlines much earlier in the week.

### Fear of Mistakes or Fear of Success

Fear is a powerful cause of procrastination in an individual's life. Fear of not doing well, fear of failure, fear of not getting recognition (so why bother?), fear of the job taking too long—these fears get in the way of our getting on with the task and become a reason for us to shield ourselves from that which we think may harm us. We use delay as a way to avoid or protect ourselves from getting hurt.

Ironically, there is also a very common fear that may be at the root of one's predilection to procrastinate. Freud called it the "wrecked by success" syndrome, Maslow called it the "Jonah" syndrome. Maslow used this term to describe the individual's evasion of growth, a fear of realizing one's own fullest powers. He said:

> We are generally afraid to become that which we can glimpse in our most perfect moments. . . . We enjoy and even thrill to the god-like possibilities we see in ourselves in such peak moments. And yet we simultaneously shiver with weakness, awe and fear before these very same possibilities.

He says this is a fear of being torn apart, of losing control, of being shattered and disintegrated by our own growth and development.

> For some people this evasion of one's own growth, setting low levels of aspiration, the fear of doing what one is capable of doing, voluntary self-crippling, pseudo-stupidity, mock-humility are in fact defenses against grandiosity.[4]

And I would add procrastination to this list.

Recently I had a conversation with a single young woman who is an assistant pastor in a large congregation. She complained of not getting much of her work done on time, of watching TV too much, and of postponing her sermon preparation until Saturday night. After discussing her behavior for a while, I asked her whether she thought her success in the ministry might have a deleterious effect on her relationships with men. She thought about that for a few moments and then said that though the idea had not crossed her mind before, she thought it might be true. Further, she was aware of the competitive nature of her relationship with her mother, with whom she was living at the time. She had thought that if she outshone her mother it might make her mother feel bad. That is a perfect example of one's being afraid of success and growth.

If you think that either the fear of failing or the fear of succeeding may be at the root of your procrastination, use the methods recommended in the previous chapter for dealing with the fears related to compulsive work. That will help you identify what the fears are, where they come from, and the extent of their power in your life.

**Postponing the Unpleasant or Difficult**

This cause of procrastination—putting off what you don't like—is probably the most common. How easy it is to forget to make a dental appointment, or to postpone calling on a crotchety old grouch, or to put off writing an article for the denomination's journal, or to delay getting started on writing a book.

When you are getting ready to start the dreaded task, you may find yourself doing all kinds of busy work rather than getting to what you know needs to be done. You find yourself rearranging the books in the library before starting to write, calling a friend on the phone before making a visitation, running an errand for your spouse before paying the bills, or fixing a frayed electrical cord before planning the next youth fellowship meeting.

These busywork activities are devices that you use because

they are *diversionary:* They provide a feeling of activity and accomplishment while giving an excuse (however weak) to avoid tackling those important but unpleasant tasks.

One of the things that I have found helpful when it comes to tackling big jobs, like the writing of this book, is to tell many people about my plans. I told my barber, the woman at the check-out stand in the grocery store, my mother, friends, and many of the people I met at conferences that I was in the process of writing a book on time management. Each time I saw one of these people, as they tried to think of something to say after we had said hello, they often asked, "How's it going with the book?" They became a force to help motivate me to get on with the work on which I sometimes procrastinate. Others have found this technique helpful when they were trying to quit smoking, or keep a regular regime of jogging, or planning to save for an expensive sailboat. Telling others about your hopes and plans is interesting to them, and they will want to know how you are doing on your dream.

Alan Laiken suggests a number of "leading tasks" that you may find helpful in moving through the busywork to accomplish what you really want to be about.[5] Here are some of his ideas as I understand them:

1. Spend a very short time on the project, like five minutes, and then stop for the day. Anyone can stand a task for five minutes. This will get you into it, and you will make some progress. We find that we are able to cut enough wood at our house to last the winter if we work just fifteen minutes per day with the chain saw.
2. Make a list of instant tasks that will at least get you started but may not take you very far down the road to completion of what you would rather not be doing. Make sure the tasks are directly relevant to what you are to be about and not diversionary or busywork. If you're going to write, pull all the books out of your library on the subject; go to the public library and get the books there; make a list of everything you know about the subject before doing the research, etc.

3. Do a detailed plan of what you will need to do first, second, third, and so on. This will help you get into the task and start the wheels moving.

4. Do something that is comparable to starting the flywheel going on a motor before you put it in gear. When I find it difficult to start writing a chapter in a book, I sit at the typewriter, put a piece of paper in it, and start to type. I can at least type what I am thinking at the time, though it may not be anything I would ever want published. I can start like this: "This book certainly is difficult to write. I just can't seem to get started this morning. Now, what was it I wanted to write about. Oh, yes, I was going to write about procrastination. Let's see now what causes procrastination . . . " and off I go.

5. Another thing that you can do to help you get going on an important but unpleasant task is to reward yourself for having worked on it. "When I get this article done," you might say to yourself and your spouse, "I am going to reward myself by going out to dinner." "When I have called on six families this week, then I can schedule a game of tennis."

**Attempting Too Much**

This problem is much like the preceeding one, except that it has not only the quality of being unpleasant but also of being *overwhelming*. Perhaps you got the great idea that you would like to write half of your sermons for the year this summer so that you would have more time for other pursuits during the busier church seasons. Or perhaps you set for yourself the task of calling on every member of your congregation, or other large, time-consuming tasks.

With this kind of problem, nothing works better than planning ahead. Break the job up into its component parts, indicate what has to happen first, second, and third. Set deadlines *for each task,* not just the whole project. You may find that the deadline really must be much further off than you had originally thought, but by breaking up the task it will not seem so formidable. The opposite sometimes happens as well; by breaking up the problem, it can be done in a shorter time than you had earlier imagined.

Your deadlines for each task will make it possible for you to monitor your progress and reap the sense of satisfaction that comes from knowing that you are accomplishing something as you move through the tasks.

**Lack of Motivation**

Finally, procrastination can be the result of the fact that you really don't want to do the job in the first place. It may be that you are in the wrong job. For example, you may find that preaching is a terrible chore for you. You do not like the preparation, you do not like delivering the sermon, and you do not find any rewards from it. It may be that you should not be in a ministry where you are called upon to preach every Sunday.

You may find that calling is very difficult for you because you do not enjoy being in situations where you are in close, intimate contact with persons talking about their personal problems and concerns. Procrastination may result from your dissatisfaction with this kind of encounter.

The cure for this difficulty may be to change jobs, to put yourself in situations where you will experience pleasure and rewards that come from the work itself.

Of course, there are tasks in every ministry that may seem odious, and from which you are not going to achieve satisfaction. You may not be motivated to teach a junior high Sunday school class, but you are not going to let this one dislike move you into a new career. Some of the things you might do that can be helpful in this regard are:

1. Make a balance sheet that shows on one column the reasons for procrastination—in other words, the things you don't like about the job. In another column, list the benefits or rewards that may come from the task.

2. Look for ways to add to the job those things that you do like to do and that you find rewarding. For example, if you must take a load of second-graders on a snow trip, take your camera with you. The chances for practicing your hobby

there may be rewarding both to you and to some of the little darlings who might learn something about photography from you. Or if you have an onerous writing job coming up, there may be no reason why you have to do this job in your study at the church or at home. Would it be possible to do the job at a nearby resort or at your cabin in the mountains? You can reward yourself as you do that which you might otherwise not want to do.

In this chapter I have described procrastination as having a number of different roots or causes. Most of these causes come from within yourself, and most of them can be overcome or dealt with by setting for yourself habits and standards of behavior that make it difficult for you to indulge your predilections for procrastination. In addition to doing the self-assessments and exercises recommended above, I would urge you to get into the habit of doing the worst jobs first and getting them out of the way. Further, you can clear time limits for getting jobs done before you start them. Thus, you can be continually evaluating yourself as you move through the process and monitoring how you are doing. Finally, make a habit of tackling jobs as they come to you rather than postponing them. This do-it-now approach can be a great help in establishing work habits that leave less room for postponing and putting off work that will have to be done sooner or later.

# III. Role Conflict

The pastor teaches, though he must solicit his own classes. He heals, though without pills or knife. He is sometimes a lawyer, often a social worker, something of an editor, a bit of a philosopher and entertainer, a salesman, a decorative piece for public functions, and he is supposed to be a scholar. He visits the sick, marries people, buries the dead, labors to console those who sorrow, and to admonish those who sin, and tries to stay sweet when chided for not doing his duty. He plans programs, appoints committees when he can get them; spends considerable time in keeping people out of each other's hair; between time he prepares a sermon and preaches it on Sunday to those who don't happen to have any other engagement. Then on Monday he smiles when some jovial chap roars, "What a job—one day a week!"

Anonymous, "What Does a Pastor Do?"

Clergy have a job that is ripe for role conflict and confusion about what to do next.

They structure their own time.

They do not have a supervisor closely observing what they do.

There is a list of unwritten expectations that they are supposed to know but have not agreed, in a contract, as to what their job is.

They are expected to perform a wide variety of job skills competently, from preaching and teaching to counseling and organizational administration.

They usually work alone in the performance of ministry and do not work with partners or peers collaborating with them or observing what they do.

They are not clear about the separation between work, family, recreation, and personal privacy.

They have very few things they can measure at the end of the day to be sure of their accomplishments.

Their job is not universally understood, and they are sometimes asked questions like, What do you do between Sundays?

These kinds of problems are not unique to the professional ministry. Mothers who are homemakers and executives in small voluntary organizations, and sole proprietors of businesses also know these difficulties. Pastors who are aware of the fact that they are not the only ones in the community who have role conflicts structured into their job will be way ahead of the game if, when they are talking with their pastor-parish relations committee or their session or their personnel committee, they do so from the perspective "These are the difficulties I am facing; I know they are not unique" rather than "Nobody knows the trouble I know."

There are three role problems relevant to time management that pastors often experience: choosing among job-related priorities, choosing between parish priorities and family and personal priorities, and keeping administration in perspective.

*Choosing among job priorities.* Choosing priorities has several dimensions. The first has to do with how much time is to be spent on the many important tasks that the clergy should be performing—how much time: on sermon preparation, on counseling, in the community, in calling, in the administration of the church. Another dimension of this problem is that the pastor does not have the same kind of freedom that an owner of a small business might have in selecting time priorities. The pastor is not the only one who is concerned about the use of professional time in the parish; there are also the members of the board, a lay leader with an axe to grind, and the folk at the community church down the street who think it's just terrible the amount of time you spend on the village school board. The third dimension of this problem is that it is not always clear whether yours is a job like an assembly-line worker where you report to a supervisor or committee on your progress and get orders from him, her, or them; or whether you are self-governed like an attorney or a doctor where, because of your training, expertise, and calling, you call the shots as to how you spend your time and with whom.

*Choosing between the parish and your "other life."* Role conflict in the ministry is not limited to the ten hours each day (more or less) that you may spend on the job. Most pastors have had the experience of having to justify to their family (sometimes rather lamely) why they spend so much time on the job, why they are home so few nights, why they can't take off on a weekend to go two hundred miles to Disneyland or Cedar Point or their cabin on a lake. They take their work home with them, and they take their family to work (assuming their family worships where they do).

*Too much administration.* This complaint, too many administrative tasks in the ministry, is almost a universal one. The cry is against recruiting for meetings, following up on assignments that were made to other people at committee meetings, keeping records and making reports to the denomination and various boards in the congregation, recruiting people for the Sunday school, recruiting people for membership, etc. To many pastors it seems as if their training, talents, and time are eaten up by "administrivia" —the many things that need to be done, none of which seems important in itself.

Jim Dittes put the problem well when he wrote:

> Instead of being concerned about persons for their sake, and instead of putting himself (as pastor) in their service, he finds himself treating them in relation to his purposes, and his

> institution's. The I-Thou relation he intends becomes contradicted by the I-It relation he finds himself pursuing. Instead of entering into their lives and ministering to *their* troubles, he finds himself asking them to enter into his concerns (as promoter and guardian of the institution) and to help to solve *his* problems. Instead of evidencing the faith and confidence in healing resources available to all men from outside of themselves, he finds himself trusting himself, his own diagnosis, analysis, prescription, manipulation. Instead of being free and open, he is calculating and controlling.[1]

## Analysis

There are three things that you can do to deal with role conflict: analyze, choose, and plan. The three activities need to happen in sequence, and no step can be left out.

The first step is analysis of what you are already doing. You begin the process by keeping track of your time in a time log. The time log is a tool to help you as a pastor identify the way you invest your personal and professional time. The essence of the process is keeping track of what you do and then analyzing the information you have gathered.

I recommend that, over a two-week period, you write down everything you do and how long it takes to do it. A sample is provided for this purpose, but you may use your datebook or other record-keeping device, if it is large enough, to keep track of everything you do in fifteen-minute segments. Pick two weeks that are relatively normal for you. In other words, Holy Week or a week in which a holiday or other special event or vacation occurs should not be used. It is not necessary that these weeks be consecutive; they can be separated by several weeks if that is best for you.

If you use the form provided in this book, in the column labeled "activity," write down every fifteen to thirty minutes those items in which you have been engaged or at the end of any activity that lasts longer than that. Indicate the time you begin and the time you finish. It is very important that you keep this form (or your datebook) with you and that you write down what you have just done at least twice an hour. If you don't do this, you'll forget what you have done and lose track of how you spend your time.

After you have kept track of your time for two weeks, carefully read the information about categories below. Then, as you look at each activity in the left-hand column of the form, assign a category to it and put the number of minutes that you were engaged in that activity in the column with the proper category label. For example, if your day began with fifteen minutes of calisthenics and then twenty minutes of showering and grooming, under "Activity" you will write down "sleeping" 11:30 P.M.–7:00 A.M., then you will have "exercised" 7:00–7:15 A.M. and "shower and grooming" 7:15–7:35. Put 450 (for the number of minutes) under II-A; put 15 under II-C and 20 under II-B. Your chart would then look like this:

| | | | II | | | | | | |
|---|---|---|---|---|---|---|---|---|---|
| Activity | Time Begun | Time Finished | A | B | C | D | E | F | G |
| Sleep | 11:30 P.M. | 7:00 A.M. | 450 | | | | | | |
| Exercise | 7:00 A.M. | 7:15 A.M. | | | 15 | | | | |
| Shower, etc. | 7:15 A.M. | 7:35 A.M. | | 20 | | | | | |

After categorizing all our activities for two weeks, total the number of minutes in each column, A–G. Some people prefer to total the number of minutes for each day and for each week, and then total the two weeks. When you have your column totals, add all your columns to find the total number of minutes in two weeks. Then divide the number in each column by your two-week total. This will give you the percentage of time you spend on each activity. (Some people prefer to use hours rather than minutes in their calculations. This is OK; do whatever is most comfortable for you.) To check your work make sure your totals account for all your time. There are 168 hours or 10,080 minutes in a week.

## Categories for Clergy Time Analysis

I. Family

A. Family maintenance: laundry, dishes, house cleaning, yard work, paying bills, getting the car fixed

All activities under this category are to be noted when you primarily do them alone. If you wash dishes with the kids, put that under I-C because it has the value of providing interaction time with them. If there is little interaction, you clean the living room and someone else does the dining room, that goes under this category.

B. Time with spouse: meals, trips, sports, talking, making love, shopping together

Put activities here that you do with your spouse alone (when the kids are doing something else). If you play tennis together, that has the value of physical exercise (II-C) but has more value as interaction with your spouse.

C. Time with children: taking them to school, helping with homework, supervising yard work

Time with the children individually or in groups (even mobs) goes here. If you go with your spouse also, it's I-D; if you take the kids to a football game, count the time in the car as well as time at the game. Regular transportation to or from school also goes here. That is a time to relate to your youngsters, and it has value for more than transportation.

D. Time with spouse and children: meals, driving to Grandma's house, family prayer, vacations

Here include those activities that you all do together: vacations, family prayer, spring cleaning, traveling together, landscaping the front yard (if all are involved—it doesn't matter how happily) are significant family time and should be so indicated.

II. Personal

These are things you do alone or with no interaction with your family members or church members:

A. Sleeping

Though you are in the same bed with another person, sleeping is not interactive. Making love goes under I-B.

B. Personal maintenance and hygiene: eating alone, grooming, medical appointments, etc.

Here put those activities you do to keep healthy and feeling good. When you eat alone it goes here; when you eat with family it goes in section I; with church members there is also a dual function, so list that under another category in section III.

C. Physical exercise (done alone or with nonfamily or nonchurch member):

Physical exercise done alone, like jogging, goes here. Team sports that you play at the Y or other places that do not directly involve family or church members go here. If they watch you play as spectators, it goes here; if they are on your team—or with the opposition—put it under I or III.

D. Hobby: done alone or with nonfamily, nonchurch members

The same thing applies here as above.

E. Goofing off: window-shopping, napping, TV-viewing, talking to neighbors, going to movies (alone)

In this category put those activities that you do that give you "space" from work and family. Maybe you like to window-shop (especially in bookstores) or read the Sears catalogs, or sneak off to a movie by yourself—those things go here. All TV watching, including the news, "60 Minutes," "Nova," and "Hour of Power" goes here (whether you are with your family members or not). TV watching is a solitary activity—going to a movie with someone else is not because the trip there and back and the discussion of the movie is social.

F. Personal growth and development: therapy, growth groups

If you are in therapy or a growth group, it goes here. Professional development goes under III-O.

G. Spiritual deepening: Bible study, private prayer and meditation, theological reflection time that is not for something else. Sermon preparation, in other words, goes under III-B.

III. Professional

In all the categories below, transportation time, preparation, and practice are counted with the actual doing of the related activity. The only exception is III-M, where the commuting is lengthy and is done regularly (like driving to work) that its significance must be understood separately from the task itself. Even if it takes a long time to get to your call, funeral, or whatever, include that under the professional activity. The reason we include preparation, transportation, etc., under the task area is these activities are "costs" related to the product. Your plumber charges for transportation time, and your dentist charges for the making of an inlay as well as for installing it.

Therefore, only a few items should show up under III-M or III-E and H. With regard to III-E and H, only those meetings and activities that are purely or significantly administrative should be there, like building the budget or coordinating a variety of ministries (staff meetings/coordinating council meetings). If you set up chairs *for worship,* put that time under III-I and not III-H. Its primary purpose is providing the setting for worship; it is not just building maintenance. If you have the building painted, that is III-H; when you can assign the activity to another product or result area, it should go there.

A. Planning
B. Preaching
C. Calling: initiated by you to take "temperature" of a person or family
D. Counseling: initiated by client in crisis or in need of assistance
E. Church administration: budget committee/coordinating council
F. Social action: attending meetings, writing letters
G. Organization-building: calling on potential members, raising money, training committee members
H. Church-building maintenance: supervision or implementation
I. Public worship and celebration (not including preaching)
J. Evangelism (not membership): helping people understand their own faith and Jesus in their life
K. Funerals, weddings, baptisms, representing the church publicly (invocations and benedictions)
L. Building church fellowship and leading personal growth groups
M. Transportation: only where there is a significant commutation not related to one task
N. Teaching
O. Continuing education and professional development

**Analyzing Your Likes and Dislikes**

Once you have logged your time for two weeks, you are ready to analyze what you like to do and what you do not like to do. This is another task in the data-gathering phase that will help you see clearer those activities you hate and enjoy. This will help you think about some of the things you might want to drop from your schedule and things you might want

## TIME ANALYSIS SHEET

| ACTIVITY | Time Begun | Time Finished | I | | | | II | | | | | | | III | | | | | | | | | | | | | | |
|---|---|---|---|---|---|---|---|---|---|---|---|---|---|---|---|---|---|---|---|---|---|---|---|---|---|---|---|---|
| | | | A | B | C | D | A | B | C | D | E | F | G | A | B | C | D | E | F | G | H | I | J | K | L | M | N | O |
| Totals | | | | | | | | | | | | | | | | | | | | | | | | | | | | |
| % | | | | | | | | | | | | | | | | | | | | | | | | | | | | |

to do more of. This is not an activity that I recommend you share with the members of your congregation. It is for you to clarify in your own mind your own priorities. Begin by filling out the next two charts. In the left-hand column of one, list the activities you enjoy doing; and in the other, those you hate to do. Let your mind range far afield. Indicate professional, personal, and family activities. Put everything down you can think of. When you have a list of twenty or so activities, go on to the following page.

## SCORING

**Activities I Enjoy**

- In column 1 indicate those five activities you enjoy most.
- Put a 1 in the box next to that activity that is most enjoyable, a 2 in the second most enjoyable, and so on to the fifth most enjoyable.
- In column 2 put an *F* next to each activity you do with your family.
- In column 3 put a *C* next to each activity you do with other people in the community.
- In column 4 put a *Co* next to each activity you do with other people at the church.
- In column 5 put an *A* next to every activity you prefer to do alone.
- In column 6 put the date you last engaged in this activity.
- In column 7 indicate how often you have done this: very often, often, seldom, never.
- In the last column put a "+" next to every item you want to do more often.

**Activities I Hate**

- In column 1 indicate how often you have done this: very often, often, seldom, never.
- In column 2 put in order of priority those five things you would like most to get rid of. Put a 1 next to the most odious thing you do and a 5 next to the fifth most odious.
- In column 3 put a "√" next to all items that you must do and cannot avoid.

DO NOT TURN PAGE
UNTIL COMPLETE

ACTIVITIES I ENJOY

List below in the first column twenty things you really like to do.

| | 1 | 2 | 3 | 4 | 5 | 6 | 7 | |
|---|---|---|---|---|---|---|---|---|
| 1 | | | | | | | | |
| 2 | | | | | | | | |
| 3 | | | | | | | | |
| 4 | | | | | | | | |
| 5 | | | | | | | | |
| 6 | | | | | | | | |
| 7 | | | | | | | | |
| 8 | | | | | | | | |
| 9 | | | | | | | | |
| 10 | | | | | | | | |
| 11 | | | | | | | | |
| 12 | | | | | | | | |
| 13 | | | | | | | | |
| 14 | | | | | | | | |
| 15 | | | | | | | | |
| 16 | | | | | | | | |
| 17 | | | | | | | | |
| 18 | | | | | | | | |
| 19 | | | | | | | | |
| 20 | | | | | | | | |

ACTIVITIES I HATE

List below in the first column twenty things you do but would prefer not to do.

| | 1 | 2 | 3 | 4 | 5 | 6 | 7 | |
|---|---|---|---|---|---|---|---|---|
| 1 | | | | | | | | |
| 2 | | | | | | | | |
| 3 | | | | | | | | |
| 4 | | | | | | | | |
| 5 | | | | | | | | |
| 6 | | | | | | | | |
| 7 | | | | | | | | |
| 8 | | | | | | | | |
| 9 | | | | | | | | |
| 10 | | | | | | | | |
| 11 | | | | | | | | |
| 12 | | | | | | | | |
| 13 | | | | | | | | |
| 14 | | | | | | | | |
| 15 | | | | | | | | |
| 16 | | | | | | | | |
| 17 | | | | | | | | |
| 18 | | | | | | | | |
| 19 | | | | | | | | |
| 20 | | | | | | | | |

- In column 4 put a "-" next to each item that you could do less often.
- In column 5 put a *D* next to all items you do not need to do.
- In column 6 put the name of a person or group who could do some or all of what you have marked in column 4 with a "-" and in column 5 with a *D.*

Before you score your list, analyze them by asking these questions:

1. What times do I enjoy most: those alone, with my family, at church, or in the community?
2. Does my time log reflect my likes and dislikes?
3. Do I do often enough the things I like?
4. If I have any activities marked *D,* how can I avoid them?
5. If I have any items marked with a minus, how can I do them less?
6. Are there any items on my hate list with a check mark that I could combine with an enjoyable activity to make it less odious? (See "Double Up" in chapter 5.)
7. Make a date to do my number 1 through 5 priorities now.

*Getting feedback from others.* In this task you are to find out what others think you are doing with your time. It is not necessary to ask what they want you to do but what they think you are doing. Ask your spouse to make some guesses about the percentage of your time that you spend with your family, in private, by yourself, and in professional activities. Then share with your spouse the time log that you have kept. Ask your partner to express any feelings about the amount of time that you put into the various activities. At this point don't do anything with the information, don't make any plans for changes; just get the data.

Now, go to your church board, or pastor-parish relations committee, or session, or personnel committee—whatever group is responsible for the supervision of and support of your ministry—and ask them to make similar guesses about your time use. However, don't ask them to discuss your private time or your family time. That's your business and not theirs. Ask them to guess about how many hours per week you invest in the work of the church, ask them to guess what the national averages are for ministers, and ask them to guess at the percentage of your time that goes into meetings and administrative duties, hospital and home visitation, study and reading, personal counseling, sermon preparation, funerals and weddings, and community concerns. (I use this list because it is almost the same as the Minister's Life list delineated in chapter 1.)

Now show them those parts of your log or summaries of your log that are relevant to your professional activity, and show them the time figures for clergy from chapter 1. Let them discuss and explore the variations in their guesses and talk about any surprises that they might have. This is not the time to discuss what they would like, only to explore what their assumptions were and what actually is happening.

There will be a tendency here for you to show off and get your board's sympathy: "Look how hard I am trying," "See how many hours I am putting in," "It's a miracle I can even walk about, I'm so busy and valuable and needed in my work." That kind of behavior is guaranteed to be counterproductive. Most professional persons in your congregation work the same as or more than you do; so you won't impress them. Hourly employees will think it's crazy to work so much; so you won't get their sympathy either. You will only be impressing yourself.

You might be interested in the study that has been done of industrial executives and the problems that they have with their time management. In a study done by Sune Carlson of twelve leading Swedish industrialists, the following conclusions were reached:

> With the exception of one man who worked every morning at his home for an hour and a half, none was able to work more than 20 minutes at a time. Most of them had thirty to forty different things to do during the day, each lasting three to twenty minutes. None had an uninterrupted period of time in which to think over the philosophy of his management and the policies of his firm. None had a long-range plan for his own

> work. Appointments were made either by the chief executive himself or by his secretary. The resulting time-table was filled, not in accordance with the necessities of the firm, but rather by the will of the most energetic or most bothersome people.

Carlson states his conclusion as follows:

> Up to now I imagined the boss as a bandmaster leading an orchestra. Now I know that this comparison is wrong, and I rather imagine the boss as a puppet whose strings are drawn by a crowd of unknown and unorganized people.[2]

*Finding out what others want you to do.* The next step in the analysis phase is to find out what the church's expectations are of your work. Here it would be a mistake to get too specific, but you do want to know what activities others think are important. Here are two exercises, either of which you may use, to get a fix on what your church leadership's expectations are:

Before your board meets for the session in which you are going to explore ministerial roles, make a list of no more than twelve professional roles that you think would be fairly representative of what the members of your congregation would expect a pastor to do.[3] Don't put in any roles to which you do not think anyone would ascribe (unless it is one you ascribe to and are prepared to make a case for its inclusion). You might include some roles that you don't particularly want to fulfill but that you think others would strongly feel should be included. Now make decks of 3″ X 5″ cards in which there are no more than fourteen cards—twelve of the roles you have previously come up with and two blank cards. Make enough decks for the number of people who are going to be attending the meeting. Once the people are at the meeting, give each person a deck of role cards. Ask them to put these cards in priority order, putting the most important on top, the least important on the bottom, and fitting in the rest until all the cards are in their preferred order. If any person wishes to add roles not in the deck, have that person write it (or them) on the blank cards and include them in the appropriate place in the deck.

Once everybody has a deck in order, write the name of each role in the left-hand column of a matrix as in the one below, and write numbers across the top so that each person can indicate priority number for each role on the matrix.

| ROLES[4] | PRIORITIES 1 | 2 | 3 | 4 | 5 | 6 | 7 | 8 |
|---|---|---|---|---|---|---|---|---|
| A. Director of Worship | /// | // | | | | | | |
| B. Facilitator of Pastoral Care | / | // | | | / | / | | |
| C. Leader & Interpreter of Mission | / | | | | | // | / | / |
| D. Coordinator of Church Education | | | /// | // | | | | |
| E. Facilitator of Parish/Community Relationships | | | / | // | // | | | |
| F. Administrator | / | / | / | // | | | | |
| G. Member of Presbytery | | | | | | / | /// | |
| H. Member of the Profession | | | | | | / | | //// |

**Priority Matrix showing the priorities of five people using eight categories.**

For example, if a person had card B as priority number 1, she would place a slash mark in B1. If she had card F as priority number 2, she would place a slash mark in F2, and so on. You will see that once everybody has put their slash marks on the matrix a pattern emerges as to which roles are of highest priority to most people and which are of lowest priority. The group can then discuss the information on the matrix. Through discussion you may find that some roles have been left out, and the group may agree to add them to the list and give them high priority. You may feel that some of the roles are irrelevant, or others may feel that some of the roles are inappropriate for your job, and full discussion should go on at that time. You may not be able to reach agreement as to whether a particular item should be in the list, but there is very high probability, if you talk long enough (and don't be afraid to have several meetings; this is very important work), that you can reach agreement with regard to relative priority of an item. At the end of the discussion you should have agreement on what priority to give all the roles under discussion.

A second role-establishing method is to ask the people to list up to eight roles that they think are important for their pastor to perform. This listing is best done on 3" X 5" cards, one role per card. Once everybody has made their own deck of cards, each person is to find a partner, and they share their list with each other. Where roles are duplicated, remove one of the cards and throw it away. Where they are different, put them together in one stack. What you will get is a list that includes all the ideas of both people. Now ask one pair to join another pair to form a "quartet." Ask the quartet to perform the same kind of merger so that you end up with groups of eight. Throw out duplicate ideas and keep one of all the separate ideas. If as people are explaining their ideas about the various roles they begin to feel that their idea should not have priority, it may be dropped, but the purpose here is not to eliminate different ideas, unless the initiator of that idea feels it is not appropriate.

The groups of eight should now write their list of roles on newsprint, but they are to agree first on the priority of the roles. Hang the lists on the wall. As the groups look over the various lists, tell the total group that your task is to eliminate roles on the various lists until you end up with twelve roles that the group can agree by concensus should be included in the list of roles in the pastor's job description. Putting this final list of roles in priority order can be done in this manner:

On the following role chart, each number represents one of

the roles. On the top line you are to compare role 1 with all the other roles. Comparing 1 with 2 on the first line, which would you choose? Staying on the first line, compare 1 and 3 and circle your choice, 1 with 4, and so on to 8. Now go to line two and make the same comparisons. When you have gone all the way to the eighth line, count the number of times each item is circled. The largest total of circled numbers is the highest priority; the lowest total of circled numbers, the lowest priority.

**CLERGY ROLE PRIORITIES CHART**[5]

| Total Number of Circles for Role: | | | | | | | | |
|---|---|---|---|---|---|---|---|---|
| | | 1<br>2 | 1<br>3 | 1<br>4 | 1<br>5 | 1<br>6 | 1<br>7 | 1<br>8 |
| 1 ____ | | | | | | | | |
| | | | 2<br>3 | 2<br>4 | 2<br>5 | 2<br>6 | 2<br>7 | 2<br>8 |
| 2 ____ | | | | | | | | |
| | | | | 3<br>4 | 3<br>5 | 3<br>6 | 3<br>7 | 3<br>8 |
| 3 ____ | | | | | | | | |
| | | | | | 4<br>5 | 4<br>6 | 4<br>7 | 4<br>8 |
| 4 ____ | | | | | | | | |
| | | | | | | 5<br>6 | 5<br>7 | 5<br>8 |
| 5 ____ | | | | | | | | |
| | | | | | | | 6<br>7 | 6<br>8 |
| 6 ____ | | | | | | | | |
| | | | | | | | | 7<br>8 |
| 7 ____ | | | | | | | | |
| 8 ____ | | | | | | | | |

## Choosing

Now you have a good deal of data from your spouse, from yourself, and from the members of your parish. You know what you do with your time, and you know what others think and what they would like. Now is the time for you to make some decisions about what to do in the future with regard to your time use. I recommend that you do this choosing by yourself, first. The first stage in choosing is to decide how you want to use your time. If you let others take the initiative, you are quite likely to end up with a list of recommended activities that are not particularly interesting to you. If this is the case, it is guaranteed that you will procrastinate, become bored, and not put much energy into your profession. Excitement and energy come from those who do what they want to do and are convinced that what they are doing fits their personality best. Once you have seriously thought about the way you want to spend your time, share your thoughts with your family and then with your board, seeking their amendments, ratifications, and approval. Let them modify what you have decided, rather than you modifying what they have decided.

As you begin to think about which activities you are going to give priority to, you need to be apprised of the Pareto principle. Pareto was an Italian economist-sociologist of the late nineteenth and early twentieth centuries. He stated that the significant items in a given group normally constitute a relatively small portion of the total items in the group. Sometimes this is referred to as the concept of the "vital few," or the "trivial many," or the 80/20 rule. The way it works is this:

80% of sales came from 20% of customers.
80% of production is in 20% of the product line.
80% of sick leave is taken by 20% of employees.
80% of file usage is in 20% of files.
80% of dinners repeat 20% of recipes.
80% of dirt is on 20% of floor area that is highly used.
80% of food money is spent on 20% of the expensive meat and grocery items.
80% of the washing is done on the 20% of the wardrobe that is well-used items.
80% of TV time is spent on 20% of programs most popular with the family.
80% of reading time is spent on 20% of the pages in the

newspaper (front page, sports page, editorials, columnists, feature page).
80% of telephone calls come from 20% of all callers.
80% of eating out is done at 20% of favorite restaurants.[6]

While these examples come from other experiences than ministering, the principles still hold true. Eighty percent of the pastor's time is spent with 20 percent of the people. Some parishioners who recognize this complain about the others' lack of involvement or assume that the pastor has favorites, both of which tend to be guilt trips that are not relevant to the situation. Eighty percent of the giving comes from 20 percent of the members. Eighty percent of the church activities are held in 20 percent of the building, and so on.

When you couple this statistical probability with the facts that (1) you can't get everything done that needs to be done and (2) your ministry and life will be greatly enhanced if you do a few things well rather than many not so well, it doesn't take a great deal of contemplation to come to the conclusion that you would be well-advised to spend more time on some activities, less time on others, and no time at all on still others.

I am not going to make any suggestions here as to what would be the appropriate amount of time to spend in the various pastoral activities in which you might be engaged. Ministries are too diverse. The size of the parish, the setting, the particular needs of the people with whom you are working, and your own skills and interests should make your time allocations unique. Further, it may not be that you can divide your ministry in such a way that you spend 80 percent of your time on any particular phase of your professional work. It is my recommendation, however, that you do seek to focus your work in such a way that you spend the bulk of your time doing what you can do best and working in those areas that are going to have the greatest value to the whole organization.

What is essential is that you make a choice, that you decide what you are going to do and what you are not going to do. But once is not enough. It is not possible for you to decide to stop doing a particular activity (cleaning up after the Boy

Scouts) once and for all. Even if you get the church council and the Boy Scouts to agree that it won't be your responsibility to clean up after them, that decision is going to have to be made at least four more times during the year. They are not going to clean up after their activities as they promised; you are going to be oppressed by their mess. Someone is going to make a comment to you about what a shame it is that the church is never cleaned up, and it will be rumored among a few (not to your face) that you have no pride in the church. Each time you hear the rumor you will have to decide again whether you will clean up after the Boy Scouts.

If your mind is clear about what is important and what you want to do, the mess and the comments will be less oppressive (I didn't say they would go away; I said they would be *less* oppressive). Further, your daily choosing is meaningful. Instead of choosing out of annoyance—"I'll show those sloppy little monsters"—or out of arrogance—"It is beneath my dignity as an ordained person to clean up after Boy Scouts"—you will be better able to make your choices from the perspective of what is important in your ministry. Vindictiveness and false pride are not valuable criteria for choices of behavior.

Look over the list of activities in which you have been engaged in your personal and professional life. From your perspective, which are important? Which can be dropped? What activities did you come up with on your "like list" that you are not doing enough of? Which on your dislike list can be dropped, delegated, or reduced in terms of time requirements?

Now make a list of all the activities you would like to have included in an average month.

## Making a Plan

The next step in the management of role conflict is making a plan. There are four things that will help you in this: (1) knowledge of your body time; (2) planning for intensity, diversity, and improvement; (3) planning for results; and (4) short- and long-range planning.

*Body time.* Gay Gaer Luce has written an interesting book on the subject of body time, wherein she talks about the various rhythms that affect a variety of bodily functions including: available energy, drowsiness, hunger, even the times of the day when one's senses of smell and taste and hearing are improved (3:00 A.M.), and so on.[7] Many of these patterns are rather regular and predictable in most people, but each person has his or her own idiosyncracies. Each person has a fairly predictable daily pattern when energy is highest, concentration is likely to be greatest, drowsiness is likely to occur, irritability or anger is likely (low blood sugar before meals facilitates short tempers).

If you observe your own feelings and behavior, you are probably well aware of your own body rhythms that are relevant to your daily life. When do you study best? Are you drowsy in the afternoon? (This has to do with sleep rhythm, not that you have just eaten. If it had to do with food you would also get drowsy after dinner, says Luce.) When are your strength and energy up? When is it best for you to be away from people? When is it best for you to be with them? All of these concerns and others that you know about in yourself are important for you to consider in your daily planning.

In addition to knowing at what times of day your body works best for different activities, it will be helpful for you to know that when it comes to studying and learning, you will be far ahead of the game (you will learn more) if you break up your studying into many small segments rather than try to consume new ideas in large blocks of time. James Delaney calls this the theory of time-spaced learning.[8] He demonstrates his point about learning by asking you to draw the diagram on page 79 from memory after studying it for twenty-eight seconds.

After you have made that attempt, he asks you to study the second diagram for four seconds and then try to draw it. Study it again for four seconds and try to draw it, again study it for four seconds and try to draw it. Repeat this six times. Most people can draw the second diagram perfectly after

## DIAGRAM 1

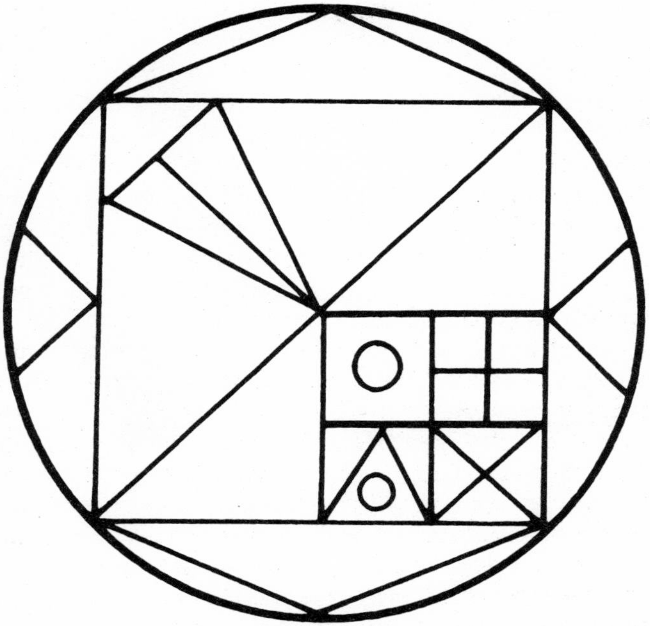

(This diagram is used with the permission of James E. Delaney, Santa Monica, CA. Management Consultant to business and Christian organizations.)

seven four-second tries with practice, while their attempts at the first diagram were less than perfect.

By spacing your intellectual intake sessions throughout the week, you will retain more and have a much better understanding of the material you are working on. Coming back to the material and quickly mentally reviewing what has gone before will remind you of (and reinforce) what you already know. After studying for a while and then leaving the material, you will give the new ideas a chance to sink in to your subconscious mind and become fixed. If you try to cover a great deal of material, you will not be able to assimilate the greater part of it.

What is recommended when you are reading new, and difficult material is that you plan to read for no more than an hour. Break up your hour into three fifteen-minute segments separated by five-minute relax-and-review sessions. When you have completed a book using this method, you will know far more than you would have had you plowed through the book in one, two, or three sessions. It will take you about 25 percent longer to read a book this way, but you will retain far more of what you have read; it is more cost efficient.

Therefore, I recommend that when it comes to sermon preparation, instead of blocking out whole days or half days

**DIAGRAM 2**

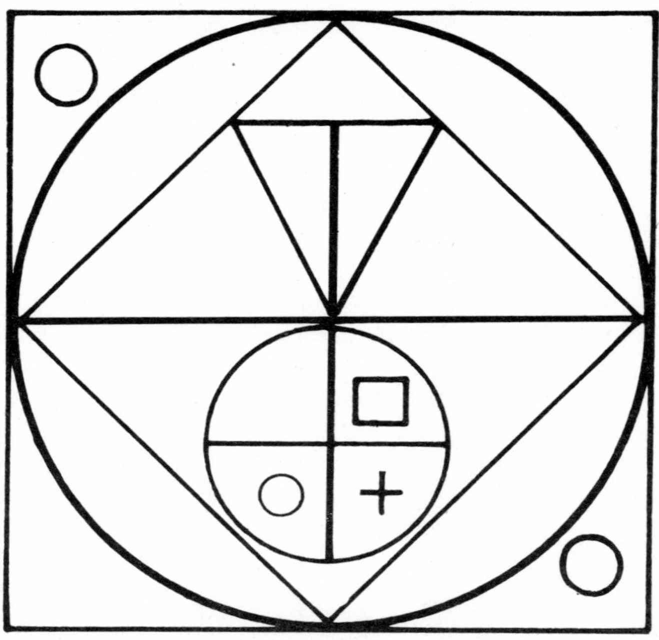

(This diagram is used with the permission of James E. Delaney, Santa Monica, CA. Management Consultant to business and Christian organizations.)

of uninterrupted time for sermon preparation as many pastors do, block out one or two hours two or three times per day for writing. You'll be surprised by how much more you will accomplish, how much less onerous the task seems, and how much more available you will seem to those who are trying to reach you. It's a lot easier to hear "I'm sorry she is working on her sermon now, but she can call in an hour," than to hear "I'm sorry he is working on his sermon now. Can he call this afternoon or tomorrow?"

*Intensity, Diversity, and Improvement.*[9] In order to enhance your sense of meaning and excitement about your life and your ministry, planning for intensity is a necessity. There should be some area of your life about which you should be intense, to which you could give more than a modicum of attention, on which you could become an expert. Some people can't find an opportunity for this in their job; so they become intense about a hobby or some group activity. But many can find something in their professional ministry to which they can give special attention, time, labor, and love.

In other words, be really good at something, good enough that you can take pride in knowing that you are contributing, in knowing that you are a valuable person, that you can do one thing well. David Campbell says: "To do this requires dedication, determination, and persistence. You cannot be dedicated and determined and persistent in all areas; don't try it, but do pick one area and excel."

You and I know people who do this in the ministry. One pastor I know is an accredited therapist in the International Association of Transactional Analysis. Another pastor who was just selected by her denomination to be the preacher for her denomination's national biennial meeting strives for excellence in preaching. Another I know has devoted himself to making slide shows of denominational mission projects (for this he not only has the fun of making the pictures but is sent to a variety of sites around the world to take pictures!).

You should also plan some diversity in your life. Even when you focus with intensity on one area, you will want to have variety in what you do: variety in your day, your week, your month, and your year. This will not only keep you on your toes, it will make your life more interesting and prepare you for the inevitable changes that you have not planned for in your life. Because of the vast number of roles you as a pastor are already engaged in, you may not feel that you need much more variety. However, you will want variety from your work as well as within it. Look again at the material in the first chapter on joining things as a way of increasing variety in your life, if you have not already read that material.

*Plan for improvement.* Continuing education and regular evaluation are important ingredients in your planning for the future and for dealing with role competition. Some of the roles in which you are weak at the moment will receive low-priority consideration from you because you are not able to do the kind of job you would like. Planning for improvement, however, can help you strengthen your competence in this area so that you can build it up so you'll be able to do the task quicker and more efficiently. Lew Towler has written a handy little planning guide for the continuing education of ministers.[10] However, the very best work that you can do to plan for your improvement in ministry is to have an evaluation annually of your work in your parish. You can take what you learn from this evaluation and then go hunting for a seminary, correspondence course, or training session that will be specifically relevant to your needs.[11]

*Planning for results.* I have found it helpful in my ministry not only to indicate in my planning the role in which I am going to be engaged or the activity in which I am involved (like sermon preparation, or worship leadership, or calling, or teaching), but also to be clear about what I want to accomplish in each activity. If I am not clear about the goals or objectives or ends I am trying to achieve by the activity, it can very likely become boring. Furthermore, I have little basis to know whether I am doing a good job according to my standards. For example, take calling. Calling is one of those activities that I can put very low or very high on my list of priorities, depending on what I am trying to achieve by it. If my purpose is to gather data about the state of the parish and specifically the particular needs of people in the church whom I have not seen for some time, I will find it much easier to do my task and be clear about whether my mission has been accomplished than if I just know that I have to make five calls a week. The "five calls a week" style can get me into trouble, too, with those who say I am not calling on the shut-ins. If I have decided beforehand on whom I will call and why, I will be able to answer my critics with confidence, and not defensively.

The same kind of thinking applies to preaching. What is the message I want to get over today? Why? What style will get it over best? These kinds of questions directed at the result of the preaching rather than at the activity will have profound effects on you as you clarify your task.

And what about time with the family? The same thing can apply. I have been working with a pastor in Ohio who has two children, and he has promised them and his wife that he would spend thirty minutes alone with each child each day. But he found that he often forgets his appointed time with the children. Even more often, when he is with them, they aren't in a mood to be with him, or they have something else to do, or they don't have much to say after "What did you do at school today?" and the reply "Nothing." The pastor decided that what was needed was some kind of clarity about why he was doing this. What was he trying to accomplish? One of the things that crossed his mind was that he had always wished his dad would have spent more time with him. He said that he felt he had not had ample opportunity to learn from his own father about repairing household items, building things of wood for the family, and so on. Aha! An idea struck. Maybe it would be fun to spend a half hour a day with the youngsters learning about items around the house in which the children were interested. They learned about toasters and wood and plumbing and house wiring. Dad and the two children spent an hour a day in mutual teaching and learning about the maintenance and repair of their property. Now they had some specific substance around which they could build a relationship that the three of them found rewarding and meaningful.

One caveat here. If you try to make all your activities result-oriented, you may miss the Scylla of aimlessness, but you will crash into the Charybdis of overplanning and compulsiveness. There also is need for times just for companionship, attentiveness, caring and aimless fun. These are not planned for. They are a gift. They just happen. The trick is to be open to their possibility and follow them when they occur. Too much planning can and will inadvertantly drive out the joy of discovery and fun.

## Short- and Long-Range Planning

There are two options related to short-range planning that you will want to choose between to manage role conflict in your ministry: broad-stroke planning and daily or weekly planning.

Broad-stroke planning has to do with those items in your ministry and family and personal life that you do repeatedly and for which you have a good deal of data from your time log about how much time these activities take. Often a pastor's broad-stroke planning will block out times every week for these activities:

Sermon and worship preparation
Staff meetings
Hospital and home visitations
Counseling
Daily devotions
A half day alone with spouse
Yard work at home
Evening church meetings
Leading worship
Teaching a class
Hobby, exercise, recreation

In addition to those broad-stroke plans, you will want to have time available for a wide variety of unplanned events and "brush fires": weddings, funerals, denominational meetings, crises in the lives of members, and serendipitous time for yourself. These times you will have to work into your calendar on a daily or weekly basis. You can't plan far ahead for them. You should have some idea, however, about how much time it takes over a period of several months to take care of these unplanned-for events in your ministry so you can arrange your calendar for them.

Now, as you begin your planning, based on your past experience and the needs and wishes of your family and parish, draw up a monthly plan of the activities that you think should be included in your ministry. Allocate a specific number of hours to each activity. Ask yourself the question, Are there any activities here that I can drop from my monthly plan because they are taking time out of proportion to the results that are produced or needed?" Drop those activities that you feel are not productive, or allocate a very small amount of your professional time to them.

Look over the plan that you have devised. Have you included opportunity for focusing on one major theme (intensity) at a time? Is there diversity? Is there time for improvement activities? Have you devised your plan so that there are variety and change of pace? Does it fit your body time?

Once you have a monthly plan devised that you like and want to live with, decide on the hours in your professional ministry, and take this to your board or council and tell them that after listening to what they had to say about their priorities and examining your professional priorities, you would like to suggest to them that you work × hours per week or per month. Tell them you come up with this figure × based on what you know is realistic for your ministry in that particular place and in light of what you know others in similar situations are doing. (Be sure to check with others before making the latter statement.) Then ask the board if the following percentage allocations of your time seem to them to be appropriate. I do not recommend that you tell them what your daily schedule is, or such specific items as how many hours you will spend on Mondays in staff meetings. I should not think that you want the board to supervise every hour of your work; so don't get that specific with them. However, you should be clear as to what your priorities are in a general way.

I also strongly recommend that you share with the board what results you are going to try to accomplish in each of the role areas over the period of a year. This can then be used for evaluation at the end of the year of your work. How much better it is to be evaluated on criteria that you agreed on at the beginning of the year (results) than it is to be evaluated on criteria that someone else made up at the end of the year. You should have two or three indicators of effectiveness in each role. Here are some examples of indicators of effectiveness. These are for one person's ministry. They may not fit your priorities at all.

## Pastoral Objectives

Pastor will spend *17 percent of his professional time* in *administrative* work with the result being:

fifty-two Sunday bulletins being prepared as well as bulletins for special services;
coordination of newsletter and monthly article;
supervisor of secretary and office work;
liason with committees and preparation for council meeting;
general oversight of the church's operation.

Pastor will spend *21 percent of his professional time* in the area of *worship* leadership and direction with the result being:

conducting and preaching at Sunday services for forty-eight Sunday and church-year festivals;
preparation of special worship services and worship folders;
liason among organist and choir directors and worship committee;
training of lay persons to conduct and lead six services a

year (including the sermon in whatever form that might be—dialogue, discussion, film, etc.).

The pastor will spend *12 percent of his professional time* in the area of *youth and parish education* with the result being:

twelve to thirty youths confirmed each year, having completed a special pastor's class in preparation for their confirmed membership status;
two first-communion classes composed of youths and parents who will have a deeper understanding of the meaning of Holy Communion;
hold one adult membership class;
teach special classes (i.e., missions) in the catechism program;
conduct special adult Sunday school classes as agreed on by parish education chairman;
serve as resource person for the parish education committee;
participate in planning and attend two youth retreats a year;
develop a varied small group ministry within the congregation.

The pastor will spend *11 percent of his professional time* in *continuing education* with the result being:

increased insight and sensitivity regarding issues of theological, social, and political import that he will share with the council, committees, and congregation;
his own personal fulfillment and sense of accomplishment.

The pastor will spend *5 percent of his professional time* in *personal reflection and study* with the result being:

a continual growth in devotion;
a reflective and sensitive spirit to people, family, the world, and the church.

The pastor will spend *25 percent of his professional time* in *visitation and counseling* with the result being:

fifteen to twenty-five couples who will have a better understanding of marriage;
fifteen to twenty-five couples who will have effected through the premarital counseling sessions a relationship with the pastor whereby they would call upon him for later counseling and direction if the need arises;
counseling of bereaved so that they may have a theological understanding of death and be equipped to cope with life;
the strengthening and help for people to deal with life situations such as hospitalization, sickness, loneliness, questions of faith, marital problems, etc.;
the extension of the ministry of the congregation to those unable to attend church;
people in the setting of their homes becoming better known by the pastor.

The pastor will spend *9 percent of his professional time* in activities related to the community, denominational affairs, and the *ministerial association* with the result being:
a greater awareness and commitment of the congregation to matters of Christian concern and service;
the involvement of the congregation in matters of ecumenical concerns.

To close this chapter, let me reiterate how important it is to be clear about differentiating between activities and results. When you talk about and analyze your work just in terms of activities, you can end up identifying your ministry as going to meetings, studying, talking, and listening. This is not a very exciting list, and it does no justice whatsoever to the meaning of your vocation. This is exactly what gets clergy into trouble when they talk about the burdens of administration. If you can connect the means of your work with its ends, you will be less likely to deprecate those necessary roles that help you develop trust, provide leadership, and make contact with the members of your congregation. Thus, as you are engaged in role clarification and sorting out what is important, keep before yourself and those with whom you are working both what you do and why you are doing it, much as the person did who wrote the objectives above.

# IV. Not Enough to Do

Resolve to be thyself; and know that he,
Who finds himself, loses his misery!
Matthew Arnold, *Self-Dependence*

I count life just a stuff
To try the soul's strength on.
Robert Browning, "In a Balcony"

Not having enough to do or not having a job that is challenging enough is not a rarity in the ministry. According to figures quoted by Lyle Schaller, 25 percent of the Protestant congregations in the United States have thirty-five or less people in attendance at worship once a week, and only one-third of all congregations can justify their own full-time resident pastor.[1] The fact that many clergy do not have jobs that challenge and stretch them is not something that is talked about much at denominational meetings, but it is a very serious problem. Four years ago I did a study on clergy deployment for the Institute for Advanced Pastoral Studies, and one of my learnings was that the reason 20 percent of the pastors wanted to leave the church they were currently serving was that the job had no challenge for them. They did not feel there was opportunity there for them to grow and develop in the ministry.

Typical situations in which a minister does not have a job that is professionally challenging are these:

- There is no intellectual challenge. The lay members of the congregation do not read, have not completed high school, and are not interested in intellectual pursuits.
- There are so few people with whom to work that to start any more projects would overly tax the time of the members.
- The town or area in which the church is located is sparsely populated, and church growth is quite unrealistic.
- Cultural, educational, and cosmopolitan stimulation is geographically very distant from the parish.
- The congregational life focuses on a tiny ethnic group that is closed to outside membership. The church will not grow because of its rather intentionally limited target population.
- The congregation focuses on a small ingroup of elderly people in a downtown area. This group is very uncomfortable with people who are different from them, and those people are made to feel unwelcome in the congregation.

**What Can Be Done in a Nonchallenging Situation?**

In a nutshell, what can be done about a nonchallenging situation is: Make it challenging. This includes two ingredients: (1) Widen the horizons as to the scope of your ministry, and (2) set goals and objectives that demand excellence for your ministry.

One of the things that impresses me about Jesus' ministry is the fact that he did not spend a lot of time nagging, cajoling, enticing, or recruiting folk who were not interested in what he had to say. He talked about planting seeds in soil where the plants were most likely to grow; he recommended that if his disciples were not acceptable in one town, then they should move on to the next. Therefore, it is not necessary for you to be consumed with the persons who are members of your congregation. Of course you will need to "pay the rent" as Jim Glasse says.[2] It will be necessary for you to provide a full and competent ministry to those who have hired you and to whom you are responsible. But it is also possible to look to other opportunities for ministry that may be near at hand.

In so doing, be sure what it is you are trying to accomplish. Merely escaping from an unpleasant situation will still leave you with a sense of dissatisfaction and lack of challenge. Busy work can keep you occupied, but it will not be fulfilling as a vocation and give meaning to your life. To the extent that you are able to set goals as to what you want to accomplish and the direction you want to move in, you will be able to feel greater accomplishment and self-actualization.

**The Process for Widening Horizons and Setting Goals**

- Choose one area in which you will specialize or work intensely.
- Set a goal to become an expert.
- Read everything on the subject you can get your hands on, and take specialized training.
- Use your own setting as an arena for study and research.
- Set specific learning objectives.
- Implement a project to provide new learning in the field.
- Evaluate your project.
- Share your learning.

*Choose one area.* You may not be clear about an area in which you want to specialize. There are some things that you can do to help you focus among many choices. One thing that you can do is to go to that list of likes and dislikes from the previous chapter. The list of likes may provoke some ideas about areas of interest that may be particularly attractive. The list of dislikes may hold some clues for you as well. For example, in one of my areas of special interest, conflict, I found that I was strongly motivated to learn about conflict because I was so awed by it; I felt so uncomfortable with it; I knew I needed to become better at it in my own personal life.

Another thing you can do is to look back on your days in seminary and ask yourself which of the subjects you took there did you find especially interesting and challenging. You may want to do more work on one of these.

You can also use fantasy to explore your inner predilections. Sam Keen and Ann Valley Fox have written a book on this subject, *Telling Your Story,*[3] that you might want to read. Here are some "guided fantasies" that might help you explore inside yourself to find those things that may have an appealing future for you:

Fantasize about specialists you know in the ministry. What do you think they do? How do you think they spend their day or week? How would you do it if you were one of them?

Fantasize about any subject or activity that is of particular interest to you in the ministry. What would it be like if you became the first expert on that subject in the country? What experiments would you do? How would you share your learnings with others?

Listen to the laity in your parish or other clergy. What is it that they are angry, confused, or upset about? Fantasize yourself helping them deal with one of those problems. What would you do? Where would you do it?

After you have dreamed and thought about a variety of ideas for specialization, choose one. Don't rush the decision, but be intentional about looking for a decision, and when it feels right begin a deeper exploration of the subject.

*Set a goal.* It is not enough to set a goal like "I'll learn as much as I can." The goal must have to do with your development and the contribution that you can make to others in your ministry. To have a goal that is fulfilling, you will want it to include what the value of your work will be for society, or the church, or communities, or whatever. Ultimately, we human beings are not satisfied with activities exclusively focused on ourselves. We want to make a contribution, we want to be useful, we want to be needed. Therefore, our goals should include some thought about what the need is and what contribution we can make.

For a goal to be motivational, it should include these criteria:

CLARITY A motivational goal is *definable* in specific terms. It is clear what activities will be required and what results will be expected. Most clear goals are *measurable* in some fashion, though they may not be absolutely quantifiable. A goal such as "I will become a better manager" is too vague and not at all quantifiable, but one that is more measurable (though not absolute) is clearer: "I will make sure that goals of this department are understood by all who report to me."

BELIEVABILITY A motivational goal is one that is *achievable;* one that can be accomplished. Some goals may be achievable, but few if any believe it. If it is not *believable* to the persons who will be affected by it, it will tend to demotivate and frustrate people, increasing their anxiety.

FOR YOU A goal must be something you want to do rather than something you feel you must do. Those goals that are set for you by others (whether explicitly or implicitly) are likely to be resisted, at worst, and misunderstood, at best.

AND FOR OTHERS A goal should contribute to the benefit of other groups or individuals. It should have meaning beyond personal satisfaction or pleasure.

IMPORTANT Motivational goals are those that are worth doing, that have value for you and the others who will be affected by them. If the value of the goals cannot be seen or understood by you, little energy will be available to accomplish them.

*Study up.* Once you have chosen an area of interest in which to specialize, look for resources that could help you know more about the subject. Go to night school. It usually takes only one night a week. You will also find many other helpful resources in the community where you live if you seriously look around. Subscribe to journals that have articles that are relevant to the subject in which you are interested. Go to the library; take home books to study; buy books of interest you see advertised in journals and magazines. Also, for many subjects, you will want to go to conferences and labs. Experience-based learning will help you become certain inwardly that you can handle this subject and that it is interesting and attractive to you. Book learning will be helpful, but your best learning will come from being with others who are experts on the subject and from observing your growth and development in competence to manage the situations that emerge in the field.

*Use your environment.* One of the things that you will find helpful in good time management is what we call "doubling up." (You will find more on this in the next chapter.) When you are thinking about developing your area of intensification, it should be an area that can be done where you are and can provide direct and immediate benefit to the community and church of which you are a part.

Your environment may not be within your congregation per se, but it should be a relevant part of that congregation's ministry. For example, your interest may be in ordination and ministry. You may be on the denomination's commission on ministry or on the committee that screens potential candidates for ordination. This is a concern that is usually not immediately of concern to the local congregation of which you are a part, but most would agree it is an important ministry. Or you may be interested in the fair-employment practices of TV stations in your community. This kind of social action concern certainly is a relevant part of a church's ministry.

Use this environment in which you are working as your arena for research, study, and practice. It is not necessary to set up laboratory experiments that are highly controlled in order to develop skills and provide usable learnings to other people. When I have been involved in learning about conflict (one of my specialties), I use each conflict in which I become engaged as an advocate, or as a third party, as an opportunity to practice my craft and learn how the experience might be useful to others. Each time a conflict occurs I keep track of what happens, what I do, what others do, and my assessments of what is effective and useful.

*Learning objectives.* As you develop your skills and get more practice you will want to set subgoals or objectives for yourself in the process. These will be items that you can make meaningful to others as you share your learning. For example, for the past two years I have been interested in learning more about power in organizations. I want to know what power in organizations is, how it is used, what its relation is to interpersonal needs for recognition, and whether power relationships could be changed in church systems.

*Implementation.* After having read much literature on power and influence, attended a lab on the subject, and surveyed a number of pastors and church executives on the subject, I tried some experiments on changing the power system in my own organization and two others with which I was working. My successes and failures taught me a lot about power.

*Evaluation.* For my knowledge about power to be meaningful to others, it cannot be random or off the cuff. I need to take my experience and place it in relation to others' and be clear about the source of the learnings so that I can document my conclusions. Some of my documentation will be from my experience: I can describe to others what I did and what happened. Some of my documentation will be statistical: I can identify how many pastors and church executives have one perception of power and how many have another. Other learnings will come from a comparison of my findings with other understandings to be found in literature on the subject. None of these evaluation processes demands that you be a Ph.D. in evaluation research. Your learnings clearly stated can be very valuable to others, even if they are not documented by rigorous scientific method.

*Sharing your learning.* There are many ways to share your special expertise. I have written articles and books and have spent a very large part of my time leading training sessions on the subjects within my competence. Next year I will lead my first conference on power and influence in church systems. This will be a way for me to share the research and experience I have gained over the past two years.

Here are some ways that you can share your special knowledge:

- Publish a newsletter on the subject.
- Write articles for religious journals.
- Contact others who might be interested in the subject, and tell them you can speak to their group.
- Contact others who might be interested in the subject, and tell them you will provide training for them.
- Become a member of a professional association that focuses on your subject of interest; give a paper there and participate in discussion.
- Lead discussions on the subject at denominational gatherings.

*Where this process has worked for others.* Lew Towler is an associate minister at Christ Church Cranbrook (Episcopal) in Bloomfield Hills, Michigan. As a result of serving on his Diocesan Commission on Ministry with responsibility for continuing education, he became intensely interested in the subject of clergy development and growth. He joined the Academy of Parish Clergy, he went to conferences on continuing education, and he participated fully in the affairs of the diocesan committee. One of the products of Lew's special interest is a small book that he wrote and privately published called *Planned Continuing Christian Education for Clergy and Laity.*

Gail Buchwalter is pastor of an interracial, ecumenical congregation in Pittsburgh. One of her particular interests is keeping the presbytery informed on issues related to social change and having the presbytery take specific stands on such subjects as farm workers, minimum income, equal employment, and the like. She also teaches church and community involvement at the Pittsburgh Theological Seminary.

Denton Roberts is an inner-city pastor in Los Angeles. He became interested several years ago in Transactional Analysis, read thoroughly on the subject, went to TA professional training around the country, and is now working through the accrediting process of the International Association of Transactional Analysis. While he has been involved in all this, he has been leading TA groups, training therapists in his church, and doing private therapy training as well. At the present time he is in the process of writing a book on the subject of treatment as the basis of operation in the church. He received a fellowship from the Fund for Theological Education and has done extensive study and writing on the pathological nature of racism as viewed through Transactional Analysis script theory.

Tari Lenon is a pastor in Thousand Oaks, California. Her forte and consuming interest are preaching. She spends twenty hours per week on her sermons and makes each one special. Her preaching has been recognized nationally by her denomination, and she is asked to preach at many special gatherings of persons within her denomination.

Ken Mitchell, who for a number of years worked part-time as an associate minister in a parish and part-time in his own consulting work, is now free-lancing on a full-time basis. He does various forms of organizational training with annual conferences, districts, and local churches. Currently he is doing a lot with Bridge Building Evangelism, a program to train local church persons to call on the church dropout.

## Other Ideas for Specialized Ministries

Here is a list of other things that might be done. The list is not meant to be exhaustive. It is meant to be suggestive, to start you thinking about what you can do to fill your ministry.

- Learn all you can about counseling the dying, and help other pastors do a better job of counseling in this situation.
- Become an expert in counseling those who are left behind when a family member dies.

- Become an expert on how the church can deal with racism and sexism in the United States.
- Become an expert on ministries to the aging. There are lots of specialites that you could pursue under this heading: recreation ministries, health ministries, housing ministries, dealing with loneliness, etc.
- Become an expert on program-planning in small churches or rural churches.
- Become an expert on developing creative programs for junior-high–aged children.
- Become an expert on creative worship.
- Become an expert on church music.
- Become an expert on ecumenical relations and the history of our church's involvement (or lack of involvement) in the ecumenical movement.
- Learn everything you can about ministering to families whose children have all left home for college or careers.
- Become an expert on raising money in local congregations.
- Become an expert on church accounting systems.
- Become an expert on contemporary literature and the way it addresses (or does not address) the concerns of the gospel.
- Become an expert on making the Bible relevant to contemporary problems.
- Become an expert on world and/or local hunger.

The problem of not enough to do is a very difficult one for many persons in the ministry. Lyle Schaller estimates that between one-fourth and one-fifth of all congregations cannot justify a full-time resident pastor who has no other employment. The suggestions that I have made here are to encourage those of you who are underemployed to make the situation as personally rewarding and fulfilling as possible. It may be, however, that an even better solution would be to negotiate with the congregation with which you are working to spend less time there and have more time for a part-time job that would be compatible with the work you are doing for the church. Careful study of your time-analysis chart, suggested in chapter 2, should be of great help in determining whether this is a good idea. It will also help you explain the situation to the members of the congregation if you would like to suggest that your number of hours per week in the church's employ be reduced.

# V. Laborsaving Devices

The items in this chapter are suggestions for ways to "cut corners" and get a little more done with a little less effort. I do not assume that each reader will find all of these ideas compatible with his or her style. You will want to pick and choose here, trying those things that you think will work well for you and leaving aside those that don't seem to fit you. The items are arranged here alphabetically so that they will be easy to find.

**Banking**

In order to save time with banking and bookkeeping, go to your bank, and ask for checks that have duplicates attached to the original. Some of these work using carbonized paper, others come with "carb-outs" (carbon interleaved between the duplicate and original). With your duplicates you do not have to write in your bankbook each time you draw a check. You can save them until the end of the week. If you file your duplicates by check number, when your used checks clear the bank all you have to do is pull out of the file those that have been returned with your statement and add up those that are remaining to balance your account.

In order to keep track of your spending for different accounts, file either the duplicates or the originals according to account name. This way you do not have to write down in an account book each transaction or "break out" your checks on some kind of a distribution column system. Whenever you want to know what you have spent in a given account, add up the checks in the file. If you want to keep a running account, staple or clip the checks together and write the total each month on the top check.

### Calling

When making visitations to people in their homes, always phone ahead for an appointment. This way you know your trip will not be wasted. The person you are seeing will be able to schedule his or her time adequately, and you will be more certain of having an uninterrupted conversation.

Many visits can be made over the telephone. Ask yourself each time you are planning to call on a person whether the call can be made by phone or whether a face-to-face visit is necessary. This practice saves gasoline as well as time.

### Cameras

Carry a camera with you at all times, in your briefcase, car, or pocket. You will find it a lot easier to copy notes off newsprint or a chalkboard by using film than by recopying them by hand at the end of the meeting. Accuracy will also be improved.

Many cameras will adequately take a picture of a page of a book. If you want to copy a poem or a paragraph and no photocopier is nearby, snap a picture of the poem using a close-up lens.

### Carbons

Copying or duplicating items will save you much labor. Get a rubber stamp with your name and address on it; this will save your rewriting it for return addresses, coupons in magazines, business reply cards, indicating ownership of books, and so on.

Make a carbon copy of forms that you fill out for insurance claims, applications for memberships, merchandise orders, or whatever. This will give you a record of when you filled out the form and what you said on it. It may save many steps later.

When you send a note to someone asking that something be done, make a carbon of it. This will give you a record that you can use to jog your memory if follow-up is necessary.

Make address stickers for those persons you write to regularly, especially banks, stores, and others that you send payments to every month (if they do not provide labels or envelopes). These can be done with carbon or by photocopying.

When responding informally to a letter that you do not need to keep on file, put a carbon under the letter and reply in the letter's margin. This way you'll have a record that you replied. If you have a copier, write your reply on the original; then make a copy of the letter with your answer. Return the original to the sender and keep the copy.

The Day Timer Company, Allentown, Pennsylvania, and other printing companies have one-way and two-way carbonized letters with your name and address printed on them. These are efficient ways to speed your communication.

**Datebooks**

There are a number of companies that make quite adequate date-keeping, reminder, and planning calendars. Day Timer, Week at a Glance, and Recordplate are three such companies. Airline magazines and credit card magazines advertise a number of them. Your stationery store is sure to have a variety on hand. The Day Timer system is the most complex and flexible. Write to them for a free catalogue describing what they have (address is under "Carbons").

However, I make my own calendars for keeping track of my time. The free ones I get from a couple of denominational publishing houses are far too small for all the information I like to keep in the same place, and the other commercially available systems don't quite fit my needs. It is very simple to design your own system and draw it on one page of whatever size you want. Then simply reproduce your form. If you don't have a copy machine, take your form to the library and copy it there. A twelve-month calendar at ten cents per page will only cost a dollar twenty. That's less than the commercial ones anyway (unless you buy a fancy binder or cover for your homemade calendar).

Commercial calendars never leave enough room for my weekends and evenings. They assume Monday-through-Friday workers don't plan their evenings. I like the calendars above because they do not end a month in the middle of a week. The way I visualize my time use is in weekly increments. This system allows me to look at complete weeks on the same page and makes it possible for me to write in scheduling to fit my needs.

The second calendar above is a monthly form that I have used. On both formats, I use two 8½" X 11" sheets put together in a loose-leaf notebook to encompass the whole form. On the first form I write the date in the upper right-hand corner of each day. You will notice that there are six columns along the right-hand edge of the first form, each with an alphabetical label. I use these columns to keep track of time that I might otherwise lose sight of. For example, column A might represent leisure-time with my family. As I look across the week I can indicate the number of hours I plan to spend with my family, and then at the end of the week I can write in the number of hours actually spent. Column B can represent the number of hours spent in calling, column C the amount of time spent working on a special project, column D the amount of time spent in denominational meetings, and so on. You can use the columns to keep track of what you feel is important.

In addition to carrying a record of my appointments in my calendar, I also carry a number of other things that I want to have in one place with me most of the time. In the front of the binder, I have my jogger notes (see "Lists" in this chapter for how these are put together). I have extra note paper. I carry forms that I often use: expense-report forms, car-mileage forms, and other forms specifically for use in my business. (Also, see the section on "Forms" in this chapter.)

Here are two forms I have made up for my own use:

Month ______________

| | Monday | Tuesday | Wednesday | Thursday | Friday | Saturday | Sunday | A | B | C | D | E | F |
|---|---|---|---|---|---|---|---|---|---|---|---|---|---|
| AM | | | | | | | | | | | | | |
| AFT | | | | | | | | | | | | | |
| EVE | | | | | | | | | | | | | |
| AM | | | | | | | | | | | | | |
| AFT | | | | | | | | | | | | | |
| EVE | | | | | | | | | | | | | |
| AM | | | | | | | | | | | | | |
| AFT | | | | | | | | | | | | | |
| EVE | | | | | | | | | | | | | |
| AM | | | | | | | | | | | | | |
| AFT | | | | | | | | | | | | | |
| EVE | | | | | | | | | | | | | |
| AM | | | | | | | | | | | | | |
| AFT | | | | | | | | | | | | | |
| EVE | | | | | | | | | | | | | |

OCTOBER

| | Date | 10 | 11 | 12 | 1 | 2 | 3 | 4 | 5 | 6 | 7 | 8 |
|---|---|---|---|---|---|---|---|---|---|---|---|---|
| Mon | 16 | | | | | | | | | | | |
| Tue | 17 | | | | | | | | | | | |
| Wed | 18 | | | | | | | | | | | |
| Thu | 19 | | | | | | | | | | | |
| Fri | 20 | | | | | | | | | | | |
| Sat | 21 | | | | | | | | | | | |
| Sun | 22 | | | | | | | | | | | |
| Mon | 23 | | | | | | | | | | | |
| Tue | 24 | | | | | | | | | | | |
| Wed | 25 | | | | | | | | | | | |
| Thu | 26 | | | | | | | | | | | |
| Fri | 27 | | | | | | | | | | | |
| Sat | 28 | | | | | | | | | | | |
| Sun | 29 | | | | | | | | | | | |

NOVEMBER

| | Date | | 10 | 11 | 12 | 1 | 2 | 3 | 4 | 5 | 6 | 7 | 8 |
|---|---|---|---|---|---|---|---|---|---|---|---|---|---|
| Mon | 30 | | | | | | | | | | | | |
| Tues | 31 | | | | | | | | | | | | |
| Wed | 1 | | | | | | | | | | | | |
| Thu | 2 | | | | | | | | | | | | |
| Fri | 3 | | | | | | | | | | | | |
| Sat | 4 | | | | | | | | | | | | |
| Sun | 5 | | | | | | | | | | | | |
| Mon | 6 | | | | | | | | | | | | |
| Tue | 7 | | | | | | | | | | | | |
| Wed | 8 | | | | | | | | | | | | |
| Thu | 9 | | | | | | | | | | | | |
| Fri | 10 | | | | | | | | | | | | |
| Sat | 11 | | | | | | | | | | | | |
| Sun | 12 | | | | | | | | | | | | |

### Delegation

Delegate everything you possibly can. Make sure, however, that those to whom you have delegated important ministries are competent and trained to do the task. Visitation work that is delegated from the professional to lay ministry should be done very carefully; your workers should be well trained, their work should be regularly checked, and regular help should be given to the visitors when they have questions or problems. In other words, delegation is not a matter of getting rid of a job. Delegation is a matter of increasing your reach through *supervised* ministry.

### Double Up

*Double work and play.* Find ways to put your hobby or other interesting, relaxing activities into the routine of your profession. If you are interested in radio, install a citizen's band or amateur transmitter in your car. Then, you can play as you travel from appointment to appointment. Other hobbies like photography, art, music, and so on are appropriately and easily brought into your work. Find ways to squeeze them in.

Start committee work with enjoyable and relaxing get-acquainted or improve-your-relationship exercises. This can be a fun learning experience as well as an effective device for building trust in a group.

Build in opportunities to rest and play around the edges of your work experience. If you are going out of town for the church, take an extra day or two to visit an old friend or see the sights of the town in which you are working. If you have friends who are also members of church committees, go out to dinner with them before the meeting (on the way to the meeting), or take a half hour after the meeting to have coffee before going home.

*Double up work and work.* Many pastors listen to tapes or do their dictation while driving about the city. While you are waiting in another person's office for an appointment, outline a sermon or read a book. If you have a report to write, try to find a way for it to have a double value. An annual report to the congregation might also be a way to communicate with your denomination about what is happening in your church. A report to the congregation on a specialized ministry in which you have been engaged might be written with an eye for its publication in the denominational journal, and so on. If you are thinking about writing an article or a book, try to tie your sermon-writing into the research for the book. For example, a series of eight sermons on death could be eight chapters in a book on death.

Double up on the use of books. Make lists of all the books you have purchased in the last three years, and ask five to ten clergy in your community to do the same. Then share the lists with the intention of sharing books. This will let you know where resources are and will save your having to purchase many books. Let others know from month to month what you are reading so that they will know what they can share.

If you are meeting with a group of pastors for fellowship and support, suggest that all of you preach sermons on thesame topic from time to time. A brainstorm session with a passage of scripture on a specific topic and three other pastors can generate more information and ideas in half an hour than you will get from five hours of reading.

Doubling up can be taken to an extreme. It can be a part of a compulsive behavior pattern—especially if you are trying to pack too much into an experience. Personal devotions are not the same as sermon preparation. Sometimes insights can be used in a sermon, but the purpose of devotions is not to accomplish a professional task. If it seems that every moment of your life is spent doubling up, I recommend that you not try more. However, some of these ideas might be helpful to those of you who have not tried them.

### Files

Keep three sets of files. One set of files should be on your desk top, either in a desk-top file holder or stacked in such a way that all the items in the stack are visible. This is a stack of items or projects that need immediate or almost immediate attention.

A second set of files should be kept in your desk or right next to it. These files are for the 20 percent of your work that takes 80 percent of your time. Such things as active committees, church accounts, and upcoming sermon topics might be kept here.

In a third set of files, keep the 80 percent of your files that demand only 20 percent of your attention. These can be in your office or your secretary's.

For the active files, keep your own. You know where things go and where they are. Depending on somebody else to find everything for you makes you dependent and wastes both your time and your secretary's.

I find it helpful to have two sets of files of correspondence I write. One set I keep. I know where it is when I want it. The other my secretary keeps. She keeps it in chronological order. Her file is there as a backup when I misplace a letter or lose the file. This way she and I have very little communication about where something is filed, and I do not have to wait for her to retrieve something.

I keep all correspondence I receive in my files. Two sets of received correspondence would be too expensive to keep.

For filing materials relevant to sermons, you may find this system helpful. Have one set of files for biblical passages, one set for topics, and one set for upcoming sermons that you plan to preach. As you come across articles, tear them out of magazines, or file the whole magazine opened to the page with the appropriate article. Put delivered sermons in the topical or biblical file. They will then be a resource for later sermon development. (Be sure to note on each sermon when and where it was delivered, to avoid delivering the same sermon to the same audience. However, updating used material is an excellent time-saver.)

## Forms

Use as many forms as possible. They help you remember what you are supposed to do and not to leave anything out. Use a form for interviewing couples about to be married. This will help you remember your agreements about the service and the setup as well as get important information for you about the couple themselves. Use another form to gather information about the wants of people for a funeral and for information about the deceased.

Make a form for every committee in your church asking them to indicate their plans for the year, including who is going to do what when and where. Even if these are not all turned in at the beginning of the year, they will be a tremendous help to you and the other officers in the church when they are turned in.

Give a stack of forms for developing meeting agendas to all committee chairpersons. This will help them remember to set an agenda and save time for the whole committee.

Use interview forms for calling. This will help you keep track of what you have done and what you have learned.

Use forms for planning worship. There is no need to rewrite all the headings and repeated items every Sunday for your intraoffice work. Even if your services do not follow the same format every week, there are many items that are always included. Make a form that allows for all items that are usually included, and then put numbers in the margin as to what happens first, second, and third. If you decide not to use a certain portion of the service, just note "none" or leave the item blank. Looking at the item will help you remember it and decide whether you want to include it.

**Interruptions**

Most time management books have a section on barricading yourself from other people. They recommend using secretaries, working away from sites that are accessible to others, and utilizing smart phrases to cut inopportune visits short. Frankly, I believe most interruptions are opportunities for ministry, and the more accommodating I am in dealing with them, the better I can hear a cry for help. If my primary concern is for no interruptions, all I hear is my own needs for order and solitude. Therefore, my advice with regard to interruptions is to look for the opportunities for ministry rather than find ways to turn people off.

Your experience may be like mine: The best-remembered times in my personal and professional life have come from events that were not planned for. Some have been "negative" events like the time our car broke down on a trip across the desert, and we spent a day getting to know the people of a small isolated community in southeastern California; other interruptions have been positive, like the time friends who live five hundred miles away surprised us by dropping in for a two-day visit.

For me, the issue with interruptions is not how to stop them but how to accept them. Instead of being outraged by friends and parishioners who stop by or call, I want to find ways to acknowledge their importance to me and support their initiative to seek me out. Getting too wrapped up in my own agendas (and their importance) I sometimes lose sight of the fact that others want my attention and care.

**Letters**

Use form letters for correspondence that is routine. In some cases these may be mimeographed or photocopied, but they may also be retyped with each sending, like a welcoming letter to a new family in the church. Having the form handy from which to type will mean that you do not have to reinvent the letter for each new family.

Reply on the original when possible and convenient (see "Carbons").

Do most of your own correspondence, especially for short notes. Every time you have your secretary type a letter for you, it takes his or her time *and* yours. This is expensive. Where a few words on an informal basis are all that is needed, your handwriting will add a personal touch and save time.

It is a good idea to handle a letter as few times as possible. I have a goal of handling each letter once. This is not always possible, but I try to open my mail when I have enough time to file and/or answer the correspondence that I receive.

**Lists**

There are many excellent ways to keep lists; some are more cumbersome than others. One consultant I know carries a small stack of 3″ X 5″ cards with him at all times. He makes one note per card on what is to be done. With this process, he is continually restacking his deck, keeping the things he wants to do first on top and those with low priority on the bottom.

Other processes, like the one you will find in the Day Timer books, amount to writing all the things you must do on a piece of paper in a column. Those things that aren't done today are moved to tomorrow's list. I don't particularly care for this method because it necessitates rewriting the list. If you are like me, there are many things on the list that will not get done for some time, and I find the constant relisting a bother. The other problem with this method is that my list becomes quite difficult to read after I have crossed off about seven items, and it is awkward to find what is there to be done. You can put the list in priority order by putting numbers next to each item, but reorganizing becomes messy and confusing if you want to change your order at a later time without rewriting your list.

My own personal way of keeping a list is to keep a stack of old business cards in my calendar that are arranged in such a way that the top or bottom fourth of each card can be clearly seen. (If you don't have old business cards kicking around, cut 3″ X 5″ cards to a size you like, use blank Rolodex cards, or cut up pieces of paper.) In other words, all the cards are visible at a glance. Some of the cards are blank, and others have reminders written on them. The blank ones are filled in as new notes are written. When a job is completed the card is thrown away. In this way, I can avoid relisting, and my list is always automatically up to date.

There are two systems you can use to display these cards. An organization in Los Angeles, The Recordplate Company, makes small week-at-a-glance books that are in a thirteen-ring binder. Each card can be punched with four holes and then lapped over another and displayed in the book. If you like, you can display two cards at once by putting a piece of clear plastic between the two sections. The plastic sheet is used as a guide to ensure that you open the pages where all the cards can be seen at once. If you use a piece of cardboard, you can only see half of the items at once.

Here is what it looks like:

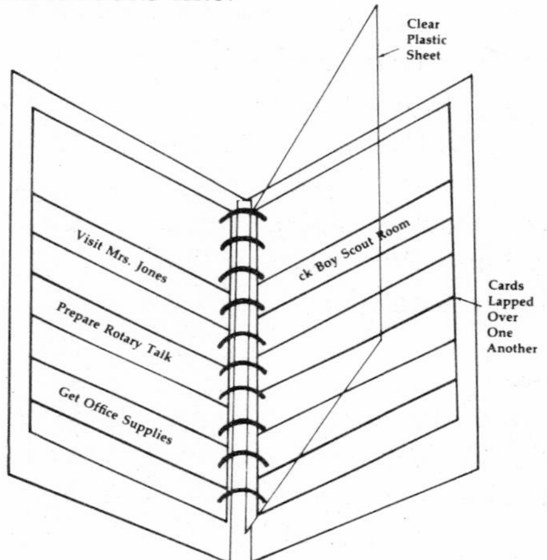


Another way to keep your notes is to affix them to one page. Take two pieces of heavy paper (the weight of a Manila folder) and place one on top of the other. Then make slits that will accommodate the old business cards down one of the sheets. To make a bottom for this pocket that will keep the card from slipping too far down, put a staple at the desired distance. This system looks like this:

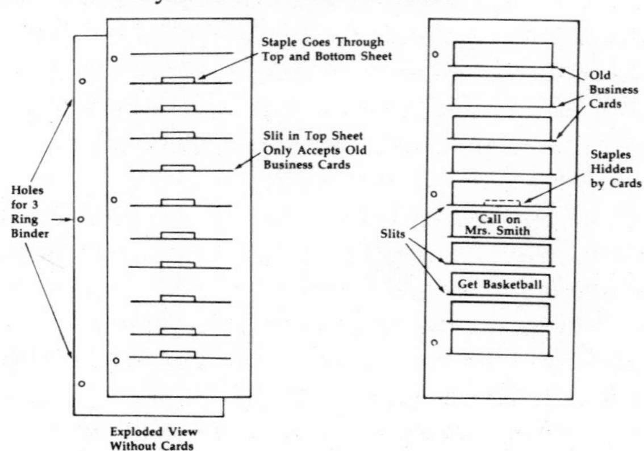

**Mail**

The U.S. mail can save many unnecessary trips and steps and waiting. Buy underclothing, socks, and other items on which exact size, color, and good fit are not critical. You can also buy tools, parts, equipment, and most anything else by mail from reputable companies. Shopping by catalog is less expensive in terms of your time, and often you can have enough data from a catalog to make intelligent purchases.

Bank by mail. Why stand in line?

Use address labels. (See "Carbons.")

**Paper Work**

*Bills.* Either pay them as received, or file them in an unpaid-bills file. Don't leave them on your desk where they add to the clutter or distract you from other matters.

*Magazines.* I recommend that you file or stack each according to its title immediately upon receipt in the mail. When you're ready to read *The Christian Century* go to the *Christian Century* pile. Stacks of unread magazines and journals don't get read any better than stacks with read and unread material. For those magazines that you do not save, have one stack for all of them, and throw away the bottom layers often, even if you haven't read them. You probably won't anyway once you get significantly behind.

*Memos and letters reminding you of meetings.* Check the date in your calendar, if it's not recorded, record it. When it is recorded throw the letter away. If it includes a detailed agenda or other important material, that should be put in the file that will be taken to the meeting.

*Questionnaires.* Decide now whether you will answer it. If not, throw it away. If you plan to fill it out, do it immediately.

*Letters requiring answers.* Do it now (see "Letters"). If it requires data-gathering or phone calls before it can be answered, leave it on your desk in your immediate-attention file until it is finished. (See "Files.")

*Form letter giving you a new address or phone number.* Cut the new address off the letter and tape or staple it into your files of names and addresses. This is faster than copying—and more accurate. Throw the rest of the letter away.

*Catalogs and brochures.* File them for future use or throw them away now.

## Phone Calls

If you have a secretary, have your calls intercepted when you do not want to be interrupted. If it is not an emergency, have your secretary take the message. Later, return your calls in groups. Plan your day so that you take regular breaks from study, or administrative work, or whatever, to make phone calls, both those that you initiate and those initiated by others. This will provide variety and better concentration on other tasks.

If you do not have a secretary, buy an answering machine that will accept recorded messages. They work beautifully, and after about six months people in the congregation will learn to accept it. Be sure to discuss this with your board first, however.

## Secretaries

*Dictation.* If you dictate, do so on a machine. This will mean that your secretary will not be tied up in the first stage of the dictation taking your words down by shorthand. It will also mean that you do not interrupt what your secretary is doing when you want to dictate. Spell out proper names. Dictate slowly and clearly to save time for your secretary. Correct your errors as you go. This way your secretary does not have to do a rough draft before the final copy. This will save a great deal of labor.

*Letters.* Correct typographical errors only on carbons that are likely to leave the office. Carbon correction is time-consuming and unnecessary. After a letter is completely typed and you notice mistakes in the body of the letter, have your secretary correct the error in the margin or above the line. Retyping usually is not worth the costs involved. As Edwin Bliss says, "The cost of perfectionism is prohibitive."

*Delegate.* Give your secretary more than typing and

copying jobs. Enrichment of this job will pay off in reducing the amount of labor you must do and give the person doing the job a sense of importance and responsibility that will pay many dividends in the work relationship. Secretaries can and should answer routine letters and put the carbons on your desk, do research for you, be completely in charge of the office machines and office budget, arrange for the use of the church building space, check before an important meeting on who will be attending, monitor projects in which you are engaged, be in charge of the church directory, and so on.

*Communicate.* Tell your secretary the reasons for what you are doing and what you are asking him or her to do. The more the secretary knows about a project, the more competent and intelligent a job will be done—and it won't have to be done over. Tell your secretary where you are going and when and where you can be reached. This will save a lot of consternation in an emergency. It will also increase the feeling of trust in the office.

*Travel plans.* Make your own plans with a travel agent. In the time it takes you to explain all the details to your secretary, you can have done the same with an agent. Contingencies that you have not thought of or problems in the scheduling will have to be brought back to you, wasting the time of the agent and the secretary. Using an agent will save you a great deal of hunting and being shifted from one airline to another.

**Shorthand**

There are several speed-writing methods currently available from your library or bookstore. I use the Wesley Short-Cut Shorthand.[1] It took me about three evenings to learn all the forms I want to use and about three months of practice to become proficient. I can now take rather comprehensive notes of lectures or interviews; I can make notes in books I am reading that are longer than they would have been if I had to write everything out in longhand, and my personal diary or journal is virtually incomprehensible to anyone but me. This is an excellent laborsaving device.

## Tape Recorders

I recommend that every pastor own a small, quality standard cassette recorder. You can use this for dictation, listening to lectures, recording lectures or the audio of a TV or radio program, and many other uses. It is best to get dictation and recording systems that are compatible. When you have two sizes of cassettes or one cassette and one reel-to-reel recorder, there are times when you will find it is quite awkward to transfer material from one system to the other. Furthermore, you must invest more money in two systems than you would if you had one system that would perform all the tasks you want done in one system.

You can save time and steps if you take a tape recorder into the chancel with you on Sunday morning and record the service and the sermon. Then send copies of the tape to shut-ins. This will be a ministry to the shut-ins and reduce the number of calls that you might otherwise have made.

Tape recorders can be used for recording speeches at conferences (with the speaker's permission, of course). These speeches can then be shared with others, and they can be used for later reflection or study on your part. In addition to taping the talk, if it's a good one, keep a broad outline of the speech as it moves along, and note where you are on the tape, using the counter on the recorder. This will help you find material later on and make it unnecessary to listen to the whole tape to find it.

Send your recorder to meetings that you could not otherwise attend or choose not to attend. This will make it possible for you to be in two places at once.

Record speeches that you find yourself giving over and over again, like the one on the history of your denomination that you give to the new members' class. You can save time by giving this to everyone before the meeting or having them listen to it before you arrive.

# Notes

## Introduction

1. Heschel, *The Sabbath* (New York: Farrar, Strauss, & Young, 1951), p. 9.
2. Edwin C. Bliss, *Getting Things Done: The ABC's of Time Management*, (New York: Scribner's, 1976); Leslie B. Flynn, *How to Save Time in the Ministry* (Nashville: Broadman Press, 1966); Alan Laiken, *How to Get Control of Your Time and Your Life* (New York: Peter Wyden, 1973); Alec MacKenzie, *The Time Trap: Managing Your Way Out* (New York: AMACOM, 1972); Edward R. Dayton, *Tools for Time Management: Christian Perspectives on Managing Priorities* (Grand Rapids: Zondervan, 1974); Ted W. Engstrom and R. Alec MacKenzie, *Managing Your Time* (Grand Rapids: Zondervan, 1967).

## Chapter I

1. Blizzard, *The Christian Century, Russell Sage Foundation Report* (April 15, 1956), p. 509.
2. Wick, *The Management Side of Ministry* (Wick Press, Toledo, Ohio), pp. 12-13.
3. Minister's Life and Casualty Union, "Just How Hard Do Ministers Work?" (pamphlet), Minneapolis, Minn. 55146.
4. Speed Leas, "Clergy and Leisure," in *Institute for Advanced Pastoral Studies Newsletter* (Spring, 1977).
5. George McKechnie, *L.A.B. Manual* (Palo Alto: Consulting Psychologists Press, 1975).
6. Kinsley, "Workaholics Are Overdoing Time," *Detroit Free Press* (Monday, August 15, 1977), p. 13-A.
7. Oates, *Confessions of a Workaholic* (Nashville: Abingdon, 1971), p. 28.
8. Ernest Becker, *The Denial of Death* (New York: The Free Press, 1973), pp. 32-33.
9. Kinsley, "Workaholics."
10. For a complete description of injunctions and prescriptions see Eric Berne, *What Do You Say After You Say Hello?* (New York: Bantam Books, 1973), chapter 7.
11. Especially George Prince, *The Practice of Creativity* (New York: Cattier, 1970).
12. James D. Watson, *The Double Helix* (New York: Atheneum, 1968), p. 114.
13. Ibid., p. 128.

14. Prince, *Practice of Creativity,* pp. 83-84.
15. Berne, *Games People Play* (New York: Grove Press, 1964), p. 179.
16. Lee, *Religion and Leisure in America* (Nashville: Abingdon, 1964), pp. 35 and 29.
17. Benson, *The Relaxation Response* (New York: Avon Books, 1975), pp. 110-11.
18. Ibid.

Chapter II

1. Gordon Lippit, *Organizational Renewal* (New York: Appleton-Century-Crofts, 1969), p. 153.
2. Sigmund Freud, *Phychopathology of Everyday Life* (New York: New American Library, 1951), p. 78.
3. Ibid., p. 79.
4. Abraham Maslow, "Neurosis as a Failure of Personal Growth," *Humanitas,* 1967, 3:153-169.
5. Alan Laiken, *How to Get Control of Your Time and Your Life,* (New York: Peter Wyden, 1973), pp. 123-46.

Chapter III

1. James E. Dittes, *Minister on the Spot* (Philadelphia: Pilgrim Press, 1970), pp. 104-5.
2. This study was reported in an anonymous manuscript entitled "Time Management." The study is Sune Carlson, *Executive Behavior: A Study of the Work Load and Working Methods of Managing Directors* (Stockholm: C. A. Stromberg Aktiebolag, 1951).
3. This idea comes from Lyle Schaller, *The Pastor and The People* (Nashville: Abingdon, 1973).
4. In this chart of my design I have used the roles listed in the Pastoral Performance Profile developed jointly by the Vocation Agency of the United Presbyterian Church in the U.S.A. and the General Executive Board, The Presbyterian Church in the U.S., 1975.
5. This idea came from John Crystal and Richard Bolles, *Where Do I Go from Here with My Life?* (New York: The Seabury Press, 1974), pp. 190-92.
6. Alan Laiken, *How to Get Control of Your Time and Your Life* (New York: Peter Wyden, 1973), p. 84.
7. Luce, *Body Time* (New York: Bantam Books, 1971).
8. Delaney, *Effective Time Management,* a privately published manuscript.
9. This idea comes from David Campbell, *If You Don't Know Where You're Going, You'll Probably End Up Somewhere Else* (Niles, Ill.: Argus Communications, 1974).
10. *Planned Continuing Christian Education for Clergy and Laity* available from Lew Towler Publications, P.O. Box 676, Bloomfield Hills, MI 48013.
11. Evaluation instruments are available from your denominational offices or from Jay Lowery Enablement, Inc., 8 Newberry St., Boston, Mass.; the Society for the Advancement of Continuing Education in Ministry publishes a fine guide for continuing education in the U.S. Their address is 85 Locust St., Collegeville, Penn. However, the best guide is published by the Anglican Church of Canada. It is titled *A Newsletter in Continuing Education* and is available from 600 Jarvis St., Toronto, Ontario, Canada M4Y 2J6.

## Chapter IV

1. Schaller, *Hey, That's Our Church!* (Nashville: Abingdon, 1975).
2. James D. Glasse, *Putting It Together in the Parish* (Nashville: Abingdon, 1972).
3. Fox and Keen, *Telling Your Story* (Garden City, N.Y.: Doubleday, 1973).

## Chapter V

1. S. M. Wesley, *Short-Cut Shorthand* (New York: Cowels Book Co., 1970).

# Bibliography

The Anglican Church of Canada. *A Newsletter in Continuing Education.* 600 Jarvis St., Toronto, Ontario, Canada M4Y2J6.

Benson, Herbert. *The Relaxation Response.* New York: Avon Books, 1975.

Bliss, Edwin C. *Getting Things Done: The ABC's of Time Management.* New York: Scribner's, 1976.

Campbell, David. *If You Don't Know Where You're Going, You'll Probably End Up Somewhere Else.* Niles, Ill.: Argus Communications, 1974.

Crystal, John C., and Bolles, Richard N. *Where Do I Go from Here with My Life?* New York: The Seabury Press, 1974.

Dayton, Edward R. *Tools for Time Management: Christian Perspectives on Managing Priorities.* Grand Rapids: Zondervan, 1974.

Dayton, Edward R., and Engstrom, Ted W. *Strategy for Living.* Regal Books Division, G/L Publications, Glendale, California 91209, 1976.

Dittes, James E. *Minister on the Spot.* Philadelphia: Pilgrim Press, 1970.

Engstrom, Ted W., and MacKenzie, R. Alec. *Managing Your Time.* Grand Rapids: Zondervan, 1967.

Flynn, Leslie B. *How to Save Time in the Ministry.* Nashville: Broadman Press, 1966.

Haldane, Bernard. *Career Satisfaction and Success: A Guide to Job Freedom.* New York: AMACOM, 1974.

Howe, Reuel L. *Live All Your Life.* Waco, Tex.: Word Books, 1974.

Keen, Sam, and Fox, Anne Valley. *Telling Your Story: A Guide to Who You Are and Who You Can Be.* Garden City, N.Y.: Doubleday, 1973.

Laiken, Alan. *How to Get Control of Your Time and Your Life.* New York: Wyden, 1973.

Laiken, Alan. *It's About Time.* New York: Bantam Books, 1975.

Lee, Robert. *Religion and Leisure in America: A Study in Four Dimensions.* Nashville: Abingdon, 1964.

Luce, Gay Gaer. *Body Time.* New York: Bantam Books, 1973.

MacKenzie, R. Alec. *The Time Trap: Managing Your Way Out.* New York: AMACOM. 1972.

Oates, Wayne E. *Confessions of a Workaholic.* Nashville: Abingdon, 1971.

O'Neil, Nena, and O'Neil, George. *Shifting Gears: Finding Security in a Changing World.* New York: Avon Books, 1974.

Sheehy, Gail. *Passages: Predictable Crises of Adult Life.* New York: Dutton, 1974.

Towler, Lew. *Planned Continuing Christian Education for Clergy and Laity.* Lew Towler Publications, Box 676, Bloomfield Hills, MI 48013. $2.50.

Watson, James D. *The Double Helix.* New York: Atheneum, 1968.

Wesley, S. M. *Short-Cut Shorthand. Revised Edition. New York: Cowels Book Co., 1970.*

*Wick, Calhoun, W. The Management Side of Ministry: A Guidebook to Help Clergy Cope and Local Churches Flourish.* The Wick Press, 4718 Brittany Rd., Toledo, Ohio 43615, 1976.

CREATIVE LEADERSHIP SERIES
Edited by Lyle E. Schaller

CLS books provide practical help in developing and administering a more effective church program, for both lay and clergy leaders.

Please send me the following CLS books:

____*Assimilating New Members* by Lyle E. Schaller
01938-9
____*Beginning a New Pastorate* by Robert G. Kemper
02750-0
____*Building an Effective Youth Ministry* by Glenn E. Ludwig
03992-4
____*The Care and Feeding of Volunteers* by Douglas W. Johnson
04669-6
____*Church Advertising* by Steve Dunkin
08140-8
____*Church Growth* by Donald McGavran and George Hunter
08160-2
____*Creative Stewardship* by Richard B. Cunningham
09844-0
____*Leading Churches Through Change* by Douglas Alan Walrath
21270-7
____*The Pastor's Wife Today* by Donna Sinclair
30269-2
____*Preaching and Worship in the Small Church*
by William H. Willimon and Robert L. Wilson 33820-4
____*The Small Town Church* by Peter J. Surrey
38720-5
____*Strengthening the Adult Sunday School Class* by Dick Murray
39989-0
____*Time Management* by Speed B. Leas
42120-9
____*Your Church Can Be Healthy* by C. Peter Wagner
46870-1

Each book $4.95, paper

MAIL ENTIRE PAGE TO:

Customer Service Manager * Abingdon *
201 Eighth Avenue, South * Nashville, TN 37202

Send books checked to

Name ______________________________________________
(Please print or type)

Address ____________________________________________

City ______________________ State ________ Zip ______
Remittance must accompany order. Please send check or money order—no cash or C.O.D. accepted. Abingdon pays postage and handling. Please allow three weeks for delivery. Prices subject to change without notice. Printed in U.S.A.